J
428.8
P672
2002

Pirz, Therese Slevin.
Kids stuff--Ingles

KIDS STUFF
INGLÉS

KIDS STUFF INGLÉS

Frases fáciles en inglés para personas que hablan español
(ESL)
(English Phrases for Spanish Speakers)

Therese Slevin Pirz

BILINGUAL KIDS SERIES

CHOU CHOU PRESS
P.O. BOX 152
SHOREHAM, N.Y. 11786
www.bilingualkids.com

OLDHAM COUNTY PUBLIC LIBRARY
106 EAST JEFFERSON STREET
LaGRANGE, KENTUCKY 40031

Copyright c 2002 by Therese Slevin Pirz

All rights reserved. No part of this book may be produced or utilized in any form or by any means, electronic or mechanical, including photocopying, recording or by any information storage or retrieval system without permission in writing from the publisher.

Printed in the United States of America

First Edition.
Library of Congress Catalog No.

ISBN 0-9716605-0-6

Cataloging data: Pirz, Therese Slevin
Kids stuff inglés: English phrases for Spanish speakers.
Chou Chou Press, 2002
165 pp. illus. Includes index

Description: A collection of easy, typical phrases arranged by activity and rendered in Spanish and English. Pronunciation is given for the English sentences to help Spanish speakers learn English. An English as Second Language (ESL) text.

1. Spanish language 2. English language 3. Spanish phrases
4. English phrases. 5. Spanish conversation and phrase book
6. English conversation and phrase book 7. Homeschooling
8. ESL 9. English language – Study and teaching – Foreign speakers
II. Title: English phrases for Spanish speakers.
III. Title: Frases fáciles en inglés para personas que hablan español
Series. Bilingual Kids 468/ 428

Order direct from the publisher:

Chou Chou Press
P.O. Box 152
Shoreham, N.Y. 11786
FAX: (631) 744-3423
info@bilingualkids.com

This book is dedicated
to my husband,
Joe,
whose idea for this book
started it all.

CONTENTS

Name:____

Received this book from:_____________________________

Occasion:______________________________Date:____________

First indication of understanding English:____________________

____

First English word:__________________________________

Favorite English word:_______________________________

Favorite English books or stories:_____________________

____

____

Favorite American songs:_____________________________

____

Favorite American musical groups:_____________________

____

Favorite American celebrities:________________________

____

Favorite things to do in English:_____________________

____

____

Favorite American foods:_____________________________

____

____

Also by Therese Slevin Pirz

Kids Stuff Spanish
Kids Stuff French
Kids Stuff Italian
Kids Stuff German
Kids Stuff Russian
Kids Stuff Angliiski (English)

ABC's of SAT's:
How One Student Scored 800 on the Verbal SAT

PREFACE

The purpose of Kids Stuff Inglés is to enable speakers of Spanish to learn English (ESL – English as a Second Language) in a practical, personal and easy manner, and at the same time to teach their children as well. This book was written with the learner in mind

The term " kid stuff " implies something extremely simple and easy. That is how we anticipate users finding the sentences and pronunciations in this book. These one thousand (plus) sentences are merely the basic framework on which to build many more sentences and expressions. The amount of those sentences is limitless.

The ease of using Kids Stuff Inglés enables the user to start speaking English without looking up meanings, pronunciation, grammar and vocabulary in order to express simple ideas about every day experiences.

Kids Stuff Inglés is for adults, parents, children, students, teachers and travelers --- all those who wish to speak English correctly in a short time.

Good luck learning English in the Kids Stuff way. Knowing English will open many new doors of opportunity.

Lo tengo en la punta de la lengua. It's on the tip of my tongue.

GREETINGS	¡ HOLA !
Hello! *HEL-oh! (or) Hel-OH!*	¡Hola!
Hello! (Answering the phone) *HEL-oh! (or) Hel-OH!*	¡Diga! ¡Digame! * (al teléfono)
Who's speaking? *Hooz SPEEK-'ng?*	¿Quién habla?
Good morning. *Gud MORN-'ng.*	Buenos días.
Good afternoon. *Gud AF-ter-noon.*	Buenas tardes.
Do you miss me? *Doo yoo mis mee?*	¿Me extrañas?
Did you miss me? *Did yoo mis mee?*	¿Me extrañaste?

Give me a/ hug/ kiss/. *Giv mee uh'/ hug/ kis/.*	Dame un/ abrazo/ beso/. *
How are you? *Haou ahr yoo?*	¿Cómo estás? ¿Qué tal?
Very well. Thank you. *VER-ee wel. Thank yoo.*	Muy bien. Gracias.
How nice to see you! *Haou nighs t'see yoo!*	¡Qué gusto de verte!
How goes it? So-so. *Haou gohz it? Soh-soh.*	¿Cómo va? Así así.
Good night. *Gud night.*	Buenas noches.
Good-bye. See you later. *Gud-BIGH. See yoo LEI-tr.*	Adiós. Hasta luego.
How may I help you? *Haou mei igh help yoo?*	¿En qué puedo servirle?
Say, "Good-bye." "Bye-bye." *Sei, "Gud-BIGH." "Bigh-bigh."*	Di, "Adiós," "Chao."
Excuse me. *Eks-KYOOZ mee.*	Perdón.
Good luck. *Gud luhk.*	Buena suerte.
God bless you. *Gahd bles yoo.*	Dios te bendiga.
Have a good trip! Have a good time! *Hav uh gud trip! Hav uh'gud tighm!*	¡Buen viaje!¡Qué te diviertas!
Take care of yourself. *Teik kehr uhv'yor-SELF.*	Cuídate.

To your health! *Too yor helth!*	¡Salud!
Health, love and money! *Helth, luhv and MUHN-ee!*	¡Salud, amor y pesetas!
Happy Birthday! *HAP-ee BIRTH-dei!*	¡Feliz Cumpleaños! *
Merry Christmas! *MEH-ree KRIS-muhs!*	¡Feliz Navidad! *
Happy New Year! *HAP-ee nyoo yeer!*	¡Prospero Año Nuevo!
Please. *Pleez.*	Por favor.
(No) thank you. *(Noh) thank yoo.*	(No) gracias.
You don't have to do that. *Yoo dohnt hav t'doo that.*	No hace falta.
You're welcome. *Yor WEL-kuhm.*	De nada.
Welcome! *WEL-kuhm!*	¡Bienvenidos!
Pleased to meet you. *Pleezd t'meet yoo.*	Encantado/a.
What is your name? *Waht iz yor neim?*	¿Cómo te llamas?
My name is... *Migh neim iz...*	Me llamo...
Have a nice day. *Hav uh'nighs dei.*	Ten un buen día. *

De la cabeza a los pies... From head to toe...

BATHROOM	La SALA de BAÑO

Do you need to go to the bathroom?
Doo yoo need t'goh t'th'BATH-room?

¿Tienes que ir al baño?

Tell me when you have to go to the bathroom.
Tell mee wen yoo hav t'goh t'th'BATH-room.

Dime cuando tienes que ir al baño.

You told me that you had to go to the bathroom.
Yoo tohld mee that yoo had t'goh t'th'BATH-room.

Me dijiste que tienes que ir al baño.

Flush the toilet.
Fluhsh th'TOY-let.

Tira de la cadena.

Put down the (toilet) seat.
Put daoun th'(TOY-let) seet.

Baja la silla.

Go get washed. Take a shower.
Goh get wahsht. Teik uh'SHAOU-er.

Ve a lavarte. Dúchate.

Your face is dirty. Wash it.
Yor feis iz DIRT-ee. Wahsh it.

Tu cara está sucia. Lávala.

Don't forget to wash your hands.
Dohnt for-GET t'wahsh yor hanz.

No te olvides de lavarte las manos.

Did you wash your neck?
Did yoo wahsh yor nek?

¿Te lavaste el cuello?

Clean your fingernails.
Kleen yor FIN-gr-neilz.

Límpiate las uñas.

Brush your teeth.
Bruhsh yor teeth.

Lávate los dientes.

Use floss.
Yooz flaws.

Usa hilo dental.

Your toothbrush is on the sink
Yor TOOTH-bruhsh iz ahn th'sink.

Tu cepillo de dientes está en el lavamanos.

Scrub behind your ears.
Skruhb bee-HIGHND yor irz.

Limpiate bien detrás de las orejas.

You didn't wash your face.
Yoo DID-nt wahsh yor feis.

No te lavaste la cara.

Your hands and face are clean.
Yor hanz and feis ahr kleen.

Las manos y la cara están limpias.

Good! Now you look clean.
Gud! Naou yoo luk kleen.

¡Bien! Ahora estás limpio/a/.

You need to take a bath.
Yoo need t'teik uh'bath.

Necesitas tomar un baño.

Turn/ on/ off/ the water.
Turn/ ahn/ awf/ th'WAW-tr.

/Abre/ Cierra/ el grifo.

Are you taking a bath?
Ahr yoo TEIK-'ng uh'bath?

¿Estás tomando un baño?

I'm running a bath for you.
Ighm RUHN-'ng uh'bath for yoo.

Te estoy llenando el baño.

La SALA *de* BAÑO

See the water run?
See th'WAW-tr ruhn?

¿Ves correr el agua?

The water is/ too hot/ too cold/ just right/.
Th'WAW-tr iz/ too haht/ too kohld/ juhst right/.

El agua está/ demasiado caliente/ demasiado fría/ perfecta/.

Don't fill the tub with too much water.
Dohnt fil th'tuhb with too muhch WAW-tr.

No llenes la bañera con demasiada agua. *

I'm washing your/ neck/ back/ knees/.
Ighm WAHSH- 'ng yor/ nek/ bak/ neez/.

Estoy lavandote /el cuello/ la espalda/ las rodillas/.

Use plenty of soap.
Yooz PLEN-tee uhv'sohp.

Usa bastante jabón. *

The soap smells good, but it is slippery.
Th'sohp smelz gud, buht it iz SLIP-ree.

El jabón huele bien, pero está resbaladizo. *

You don't need so much:
soap, (*sohp*)
water, (*WAW-tr*)
toothpaste, *(TOOTH-peist)*
deodorant, *(dee-OH-d'r-ent)*
make-up. *(MEIK-uhp)*

No necesitas tanto:
jabón,
agua,
pasta de dientes,
desodorante,
maquillaje.

Dry yourself well.
Drigh yor-SELF wel.

Sécate bien.

/Empty/ Clean/ the bathtub.
/EMP-tee/ Kleen/ th'BATH-tuhb.

/Vacía / Limpia/ la bañera.

Fold the towel.
Fohld th'taoul.

Dobla la toalla. *

Put the towel in the laundry.
Put th'taoul in th'LAWN-dree.

Pon la toalla en la lavadora.

Hang up the face cloth.
Hang ahp th'feis klawth.

Cuelga la toallita de la cara.

Did you turn off the light?
Did yoo turn awf th'light?

¿Apagaste la luz?

Do you like to take a bath?
Doo yoo lighk t'teik uh'bath?

¿Te gusta el baño?

Yes. I like it.
Yes. Igh lighk it.

Sí. Me gusta.

The bathroom belongs to the whole family!
Th'BATH-room bee-LAWNGZ t'th'hohl FAM-lee!

¡La sala de baño es de toda la familia!

I think you need to shave.
Igh think yoo need t'sheiv.

Creo que tú tienes que afeitarte. *

Wash your hair later.
Wahsh yor hehr LEI-tr.

Lávate el pelo más tarde.

Me sienta como un guante. It's fits like a glove.

GETTING DRESSED	VESTIRSE
Did you sleep well? *Did yoo sleep wel?*	¿Dormiste bien?
Get up! It's time to wake up! *Get ahp! Itz tighm t'weik ahp!*	¡Levantate! ¡Es hora de despertarte!
I'm changing your diaper. *Ighm CHEINJ- 'ng yor DIGH-pr.*	Estoy cambiandote el pañal.
Put your hand in the sleeve *Put yor hand in th'sleev.*	Mete la mano dentro de la manga.
Put your foot into your pants. *Put yor fut IN-too yor pantz.*	Mete el pie en los pantalones. *
I'm putting your right foot into your right shoe. *Ighm PUT- 'ng yor right fut IN-too yor right shoo.*	Estoy metiendote el pie derecho en el zapato derecho. *
You put your foot into the wrong shoe. *Yoo put yor fut IN-too th'rawng shoo.*	Metiste el pie en el zapato contrario.

Take your arm out of the sleeve.
Teik yor ahrm aout uhv'th'sleev.

Saca el brazo de la manga.

I'm putting on your pajamas.
Ighm PUT- 'ng ahn yor pah-JAIIM-ahs.

Yo te estoy poniendo el pijama.

Go get your shoes.
Goh get yor shooz.

Busca tus zapatos.

I'm missing a shoe.
Ighm MIS- 'ng uh'shoo.

Me falta un zapato.

Button your shirt
BUH-tun yor shirt.

Abrochate tu camisa. *

Do you want to wear the blue blouse or the red one?
Doo yoo wahnt t'wehr th'bloo blaous or th'red wuhn?

¿Quieres ponerte la blusa azul o la roja?

Where is your hat?
Wehr iz yor hat?

¿Dónde está tu sombrero?

Close the zipper of your jacket.
Klohz th'ZIP-er uhv'yor JAK-et.

Cierra la cremallera de tu chaqueta.
* *

Look for your gloves.
Luk for yor gluhvz.

Busca tus guantes. *

Daddy has gone to work.
DAD-ee haz gahn t'wurk.

Papá se fue al trabajo.

Get dressed.
Get drest.

Vístete.

We must get dressed.
Wee muhst get drest.

Tenemos que vestirnos.

Don't bite your (finger)nails.
Dohnt bight yor (FIN-gr)neilz.

No te muerdas las uñas.

VESTIRSE

Put on your underwear and your pants.
Put ahn yor UHN-der-wehr and yor pantz.

Ponte la ropa interior y los pantalones.

Put on (Wear) your new coat.
Put ahn (Wehr) yor nyoo koht.

Ponte tu abrigo nuevo.

Let me help you tie your shoelace.
Let mee help yoo tigh yor shoo-leis.

Déjame ayudarte a atar el cordón del zapato. *

There is a knot in your shoelace.
Thehr iz uh'naht in yor shoo-leis.

Hay un nudo en el cordón del zapato.

Comb your hair.
Kohm yor hehr.

Péinate.

Brush your hair.
Bruhsh yor hehr.

Cepilla tu pelo.

The brush, comb and nail file are on the dresser.
Th'bruhsh, kohm and neil fighl ahr ahn th' DRES-er.

El cepillo, el peine y la lima están en la cómoda. *

The T-shirt will be fine.
Th'TEE-shirt wil bee fighn.

La camiseta está bien.

MEAL TIME — HORA de COMER

Let's eat! *Letz eet!*	¡Comamos!
Do you want breakfast? *Doo yoo wahnt BREK-fest?*	¿Quieres el desayuno?
Come and get your cereal. *Kuhm and get yor SEER-ee-ul.*	Ven y come tu cereal.
When are we having lunch? *Wen ahr wee HAV-'ng luhnch?*	¿A que hora almorzamos?
I'm / hungry/ thirsty/. *Ighm/ HUHNG-ree/ THURS-tee/.*	Tengo/ hambre/ sed/.
What do you want to eat? *Waht doo yoo wahnt t'eet?*	¿Qué quieres comer?
Would you like some more? *Wud yoo lighk suhm mor?*	¿Te sirvo más?

Something else? *SUHM-thing els?*	¿Algo más?
You have not eaten (anything) all day. *Yoo hav naht EE-'tn (EN-ee-thing) awl dei.*	No has comido (nada) en todo el día.
Dinner is ready. Sit down. *DIN-er iz RED-ee. Sit daoun.*	La cena está lista. Siéntate.
Sit close to the table. *Sit klohs t'th'TEI-bl.*	Siéntate cerca de la mesa.
Don't put your elbows on the table. *Dohnt put yor EL-bohz ahn th'TEI-bl.*	No pongas los codos en la mesa.
You shouldn't talk with your mouth full. *Yoo SHUD-'nt tawk with yor maouth ful.*	No debes hablar con la boca llena.
Would you like a nice snack? *Wud yoo lighk uh'nighs snak?*	¿Quieres una merienda rica?
Do you want bacon or potatoes? *Doo yoo wahnt BEI-k'n or poh-TEI-tohz?*	¿Quieres tocino o papas?
Help yourself. *Help yor-SELF.*	Sírvete.
Fix yourself a sandwich. *Fix yor-SELF uh'SAND-wich.*	Hazte un sándwich.
May I have more carrots? *Mei igh hav mor KAR-utz?*	¿Puedo tener más zanahorias?
Do you want more? *Doo yoo wahnt mor?*	¿Quieres más?
Would you like more? *Wud yoo lighk mor?*	¿Querrías más?
Is there any more left for me? *Iz thehr EN-ee mor left for mee?*	¿Queda más para mí?

I'll take a little more cereal. *Ighl teik uh'LIT-le mor SEER-ee-ul.*	Tomaré un poco más de cereal.
I don't want any more. *Igh dohnt wahnt EN-ee mor.*	No quiero más.
I already have enough. *Igh awl-RED-ee hav ih-NUHF.*	Ya tengo bastante.
May I taste (your ice cream)? *Mei igh teist (yor ighs kreem)?*	¿Me dejas probar (tu helado)?
I cannot eat any more. *Igh kan-NAHT eet EN-ee mor.*	No puedo comer más.
This is all I have. *This iz awl igh hav.*	No tengo más de esto.
Pass the salt, please. *Pas th'sawlt, pleez.*	Pásame la sal, por favor. *
Use your fork, knife, spoon. *Yooz yor fork, nighf, spoon.*	Usa tu tenedor, cuchillo, cucharita.
Don't squeeze the banana in your hand. *Dohnt skweez th'buh-NAN-uh in yor hand.*	No aprietes el plátano en tu mano. *
Eat the ripe apple, but be careful of the pits. *Eet th'righp AP'le, buht bee KEHR-ful uhv'th'pitz.*	Come la manzana madura, pero ten cuidado con las semillas. *
Let me cut your meat. *Let mee kuht yor meet.*	Déjame cortar la carne.
Would anyone like hot dogs? *Wud EN-ee-wuhn lighk haht dawgz?*	¿Alguien quiere perritos calientes? *
Don't drink your milk so fast. *Dohnt drink yor milk soh fast.*	No tomes la leche con tanta prisa.
Eat just a little. *Eet juhst uh'LIT-le.*	Solamente come un poco.

The food smells so good.
Th'food smelz soh gud.

Qué aroma tan bueno.

It is sour.
It iz saour.

Es agrio/ a/.

The coffee is bitter.
Th'KAWF-ee iz BIT-er.

El café es amargo.

The dessert is sweet.
Th'dis-ERT iz sweet.

El postre es dulce. *

The sauce is bland.
Th'saws iz bland.

La salsa es muy blanda.

The fish is too salty.
Th'fish iz too SAWL-tee.

El pescado está demasiado salado. *

The steak is juicy.
Th'steik iz JOO-see.

El biftec es jugoso.

Do you like cheese?
Doo yoo lighk cheez?

¿Te gusta el queso?

Would you like a sip of tea?
Wud yoo lighk uh'sip uhv'tee?

¿Te gustaría un sorbito de té?

Eat your spinach.
Eet yor SPIN-ech.

Come tus espinacas.

I like stringbeans.
Igh lighk STRING-beenz.

Me gustan las judías verdes. *

You can feed yourself. Try it.
Yoo kan feed yor-SELF. Trigh it.

Puedes comer solo/ a. Inténtalo.

You have food all over your face.
Yoo hav food awl OH-ver yor feis.

Tienes comida en toda la cara.

Don't speak with your mouth full.
Dohnt speek with yor maouth ful.

No hables con la boca llena.

Pour the milk in the glass.
Por th'milk in th'glas.

Sirve la leche en el vaso.

Someone left some milk in the glass.
SUHM-wuhn left suhm milk in th'glas.

Alguien dejó un poco de leche en el vaso.

Cut the bread carefully.
Kuht th'bred KEHR-fuh-lee.

Corta el pan con cuidado. *

Don't fill the glass.
Dohnt fil th'glas.

No llenes el vaso.

Don't spill the water.
Dohnt spil th'WAHW-ter.

No desparrames el agua.

Why must you eat so much?
Wigh muhst yoo eet soh muhch?

¿Por qué tienes que comer tanto?

Finish your juice.
FIN-ish yor joos.

Toma todo el jugo.

Will you give me a bite?
Wil yoo giv mee uh'bight?

¿Podrás darme un bocado?

Have you finished eating?
Hav yoo FIN-isht EET-'ng?

¿Has terminado de comer?

All gone.
Awl gahn.

Eso es todo.

Oh! How delicious!
Oh! Haou dih-LISH-uhs!

¡Ay! ¡Qué rico/ a!

You have eaten everything on your plate.
Yoo hav EET-en EV-ree-thing ahn yor pleit.

Comiste todo lo que estaba en el plato.

Enjoy your meal!
En-JOY yor meel!

¡Buen provecho!

What a good meal!
Waht uh'gud meel!

¡Qué buena cena!

CONVERSATION	CONVERSACIÓN

What is/ that/ this/?
Waht iz/ that/ this/?

¿Qué es /eso/ esto/?

It's a horse.
Itz uh'hors.

Es un caballo.

What do you hear?
Waht doo yoo heer?

¿Qué oyes?

What a (terrible) noise!
Waht uh (TER-ih-bl) noyz!

¡Qué ruido (espantoso)!

Did I frighten you?
Did igh FRIGHT-en yoo?

¿Te he asustado?

Come on!
Kuhm ahn!

¡Vamos!

What are you saying?
Waht ahr yoo SEI-'ng?

¿Qué dices?

What did you say?
Waht did yoo sei?

¿Qué dijiste?

I'm listening (to you).
Ighm LIS-'ng (too yoo).

Yo (te) escucho.

How well you sing!
Haou wel yoo sing!

¡Qué bien cantas!

How talkative you are!
Haou TAWK-uh-tiv yoo ahr!

¡Qué hablador/a/ eres! (m/f)

Sit up (straight)!
Sit ahp (streit)!

¡Siéntate (recto/ a)!

Sit on my lap.
Sit ahn migh lap.

Siéntate en mi regazo.

Raise your head
Reiz yor hed.

Levanta la cabeza.

Look how strong!
Luk haou strawng!

¡Mira, qué fuerte!

Hold it!
Hohld it!

¡Ten!

Hold the rattle!
Hohld th'RAT-le!

¡Ten el sonajero!

Let go!
Let goh!

¡Deja!

What are you looking at?
Waht ahr yoo LUK-'ng at?

¿Qué miras?

What are you thinking about?
Waht ahr yoo THINK-'ng uh-BAOUT?

¿Qué piensas?

I can see that you are dreaming.
Igh kan see that yoo ahr DREEM-'ng.

Yo veo que tú estás soñando.

CONVERSACIÓN

Move your arms and legs. *Moov yor ahrmz and legz.*	Mueve los brazos y las piernas.
Who am I? *Hoo am igh?*	¿Quién soy?
Who is it? *Hoo iz it?*	¿Quién es?
I know you. *Igh noh yoo.*	Yo te conozco.
It's your/ brother/ sister/. *Itz yor/ BRUTH-er/ SIS-ter/.*	Es tu/ hermano/ hermana/.
He is small. *Hee iz smawl.*	El es pequeño.
She is small. *Shee iz smawl.*	Ella es pequeña.
It is/ large/ small/. *It iz/ lahrj/ smawl/.*	Es /grande/ pequeña/.
You have eyes like Daddy's. *Yoo hav ighz lighk DAD-eez.*	Tú tienes ojos como papá.
Smile! *Smighl!*	¡Sonrie!
Show me a big smile. *Shoh mee uh'big smighl.*	Muéstrame una sonrisa grande.
Here is your nose, your mouth, your ear. *Heer iz yor nohz, yor maouth, yor ir.*	Aquí está tu nariz, tu boca, tu oreja.
I want to take your picture. *Igh wahnt t'teik yor PIK-chur.*	Quiero sacarte una foto. *
Put a smile on your face! *Put uh'smighl ahn yor feis!*	¡Alégrate esa cara!

What a pretty story!
Waht uh'PRIH-tee STOR-ee!

¡Qué cuento lindo!

You like that, don't you?
Yoo lighk that, dohnt yoo?

A tí te gusta eso ¿verdad?

Let me massage your tummy.
Let mee mah-SAHJ yor TUM-ee.

Déjame darte un masaje en el estómago.

Where are you going?
Wehr ahr yoo GOH-'ng?

¿Adónde vas?

Be quick!
Bee kuik!

¡Date prisa!

Not so fast!
Naht soh fast!

¡No tan rápido!

Get up.
Get ahp.

Levántate.

Stand on your feet
Stand ahn yor feet.

Estate de pie.

Roll over.
Rohl OH-ver.

Date vuelta.

Do you see...?
Doo yoo see...?

¿Ves...?

Can you hold the mouse?
Kan yoo hohld th'maous?

¿Puedes tener el mouse? *

What do you have in your /mouth/ hand/?
Waht doo yoo hav in yor/ maouth/ hand/?

¿Qué tienes en la / boca/ mano/?

Don't put that in your mouth.
Dohnt put that in yor maouth.

No pongas eso en la boca. *

Give it to me.
Giv it too mee.

Dámelo.

CONVERSACIÓN

No kicking! *Noh KIK-'ng!*	¡No des patadas!
No splashing! *Noh SPLASH-'ng!*	¡No hagas saltar el agua!
How you kick! *Haou yoo kik!*	¡Cómo das patadas!
You're getting me wet! *Yor GET-'ng mee wet!*	¡Me estás mojando!
Don't cry. It's O.K. *Dohnt krigh. Itz oh-kei.*	No llores. Está bien.
Why are you crying? *Wigh ahr yoo KRIGH-'ng?*	¿Por qué lloras?
Who's that in the mirror? *Hooz that in th'MIR-er?*	¿Quién es ese en el espejo? *
Who loves you? *Hoo luhvz yoo?*	¿Quién te ama?
Do you want to play with the ball? *Doo yoo wahnt t'plei with th'bawl?*	¿Te gustaría jugar a la pelota? *
Here it is. *Heer it iz.*	Aquí está.
We're going to visit grandma. *Weer GOH-'ng t'VIZ-it GRAND-mah.*	Vamos a visitar a la abuelita.
Get ready to go out. *Get RED-ee t'goh aout.*	Preparate para salir.
We're going to show her how big you are. *Weer GOH-'ng t'shoh her haou big yoo ahr*	Nosotros vamos a mostrarle cómo estás de grande.
I want to see/ him/ her/. *Igh wahnt t'see/ him/ her/.*	Quiero verlo/-la/.

Come to Mommy.
Kuhm t'MAH-mee.

Ven a mami.

Let's see how you walk.
Letz see haou yoo wawk.

Vamos a ver como caminas.

Look at those teeth!
Luk at thohz teeth!

¡Mira esos dientes!

Do your teeth hurt?
Doo yor teeth hurt?

¿Te duelen los dientes?

Not so loud!
Naht soh laoud!

¡No tan fuerte!

Don't shout!
Dohnt shaout!

¡No des voces!

Play the drum! Ring the bell!
Plei th'drum! Ring th'bel!

¡Toca el tambor! ¡Toca la *
campanilla!

Play another song!
Plei uh-NUTH-er sawng!

¡Toca otra canción!

Clap! What beautiful music!
Klap! What BYOO-tih-ful MYOO-zik!

¡Aplaude! ¡Qué música más bonita!
*

Here is a baby like you.
Heer iz uh'BEI-bee lighk yoo.

Aquí hay un bebé como tú.

Where are the feet (of the baby)?
Wehr ahr th'feet (uv'th'BEI-bee)?

¿Dónde están los pies (del bebé)?

Let's take a stroll in your carriage.
Letz teik uh'strohl in yor KAR-ij.

Vamos a dar un paseo en tu coche.

We have to go to the doctor's office.
Wee hav t'goh t'th'DAHK-terz AWF-ihs.

Tenemos que ir a la oficina del
médico.

It's time for a check-up.
Itz tighm for uh'CHEK-ahp.

Es la hora del reconocimiento.

CONVERSACIÓN

Don't be afraid. *Dohnt bee uh-FREID.*	No tengas miedo.
Mommy is here. *MAH-mee iz heer.*	Mami está aquí.
I'm coming. *Ighm KUHM-'ng.*	Aquí vengo.
I'm going to get you! *Ighm GOH-'ng t'get yoo!*	¡Te voy a coger!
Got-cha! *GAHT-chuh!*	¡Te cogí!
Don't you like...? *Dohnt yoo lighk...?*	¿No te gusta..? ¿No te gustan...?
Let's take a little walk. *Letz teik uh'LIT-le wawk.*	Vamos a caminar un poco.
Take my hand. *Teik migh hand.*	Toma mi mano.
Sit in the chair. *Sit in th'chehr.*	Siéntate en la silla. *
Stay (there) in your seat. *Stei (thehr) in yor seet.*	Quédate (allí) en el asiento.
Watch the step. *Wahch th'step.*	Cuidado con el escalón.
Climb the stairs. *Klighm th'stehrz.*	Sube la escalera. *
Sit on the landing. *Sit ahn th'LAND-'ng.*	Siéntate sobre el descansillo.
Don't turn around. *Dohnt turn uh-RAOUND.*	No te des vuelta.

Come down the stairs.
Kuhm daoun th'stehrz.

Baja la escalera.

Jump! Don't jump!
Jump! Dohnt jump!

¡Salta! ¡No Saltes!

Give it to daddy.
Giv it t'DAD-ee.

Dáselo a papi.

Give it to daddy.
Giv it t'DAD-ee.

Dásela a papi.

Let go of it.
Let goh uhv'it.

Suéltalo.

Give it (m) to me.
Giv it t' mee.

Dámelo.

Don't touch. Don't break it.
Dohnt tuhch. Dohnt breik it.

No toques. No lo rompas.

That doesn't go there.
That DUHZ-nt goh thehr.

Eso no va allí.

Reach for the block.
Reech for th'blahk.

Alcanza el cubo. *

Feed your doll.
Feed yor dahl.

Dale de comer a tu muñeca.

Take good care of Teddy.
Teik gud kehr uhv'TEH-dee.

Cuída bien a Tedi. *

Give/ her/ him/ some tea.
Giv/ her/ him/ suhm tee.

Dale té.

Pet the dog gently.
Pet th'dawg JEHNT-lee.

Hazle caricias al perro suavemente. *

Don't make so much noise.
Dohnt meik soh muhch noyz.

No hagas tanto ruido.

That hurts (me). *That hurtz (mee).*	Eso (me) duele.
Stop: *Stahp*:	Deja de:
kicking, *KIK-'ng,*	patear,
hitting, *HIT-'ng,*	pegar,
biting, *BIGHT-'ng,*	morder,
crying. *KRIGH-'ng.*	llorar.
Stop! Enough! *Stahp! Ih-NUHF!*	¡Basta!
No: *Noh*:	No:
kicking, *KIK-'ng,*	des patadas,
hitting, *HIT-'ng,*	pegues,
biting, *BIGHT-'ng,*	muerdas,
crying, *KRIGH-'ng.*	llores,
eating. *EET-'ng.*	comas.
Don't go in! No admittance! *Dohnt goh in! Noh ad-MIHT-tehns!*	¡No entres!

Give me your hand. *Giv mee yor handz.*	Dame la mano.
Don't give me... *Dohnt giv mee...*	No me des...
Come and whisper in my ear. *Kuhm and WIS-per in migh ir.*	Ven y dilo a mi oído.
I'm all ears. *Ighm awl irz.*	Soy todo oídos.
Quiet, please. *KWIGH-et, pleez.*	Silencio, por favor.
Lower your voice. *LOH-er yor voys.*	Baja tu voz.
Be quiet! Shut up! (Coarse language) *Bee KWIGH-et! Shut ahp!*	¡Callate!
Don't ask me again. *Dohnt ask mee uh-GEN.*	No me preguntes otra vez.
I'm busy now. *Ighm BIZ-ee naou.*	Estoy ocupado/-a /ahora.
I'm in a hurry. *Ighm in uh'HUR-ee.*	Tengo prisa.
I must go. *Igh muhst goh.*	Tengo que irme.
We have to hurry. *Wee hav t'HUR-ee.*	Tenemos que darnos prisa.
We must go. *Wee muhst goh.*	Tenemos que irnos.
I'll come back later. *Ighl kuhm bak LEI-tr.*	Vuelvo más tarde.

CONVERSACIÓN

I'm coming in a moment. *Ighm KUHM-'ng in uh'MOH-ment.*	Vengo en un momento.
Wait! (until I come back). *Weit! (uhn-TIL igh kuhm bak).*	¡Espera! (hasta que vuelva).
Don't move. *Dohnt moov.*	No te muevas.
Don't go away. *Dohnt goh uh-WEI.*	No te vayas.
Stop! (in place) *Stahp! (in pleis)*	¡Para!
Stop doing that. *Stahp DOO-'ng that.*	Deja de hacerlo.
Come away from there. *Kuhm uh-WEI fruhm thehr.*	Sal de allí.
Do as I tell you! *Doo az igh tel yoo!*	¡Haz lo que te digo!
And right away! *And right uh-WEI!*	¡Y enseguida!
Do what you like. *Doo waht yoo lighk.*	Haz lo que quieras.
Let's talk about this later. *Letz tawk uh-BAOUT this LEI-tr.*	Hablaremos sobre esto más tarde.
Is it to my liking? Would I like it? *Iz it too migh LIGHK-'ng? Wud igh lighk it?*	¿Es de mi agrado?
Don't give me trouble. *Dohnt giv mee TRUH-bl.*	No me des problemas.
Don't disobey me. *Dohnt dis-oh-BEI mee.*	No me desobedezcas.

Take turns! *Teik turnz!*	¡Por turnos!
Don't quarrel with one another. *Dohnt KWAHR-el with wuhn uh-NUH-ther.*	No se peleen.
Leave/ him/ her/ alone. *Leev/ him/ her/ uh-LOHN.*	Déjalo/a quieto/a/.
Leave the cat alone. Don't tease him. *Leev th'kat uh-LOHN. Dohnt teez him.*	Deja el gato. No le molestes.
Leave that alone. Stop that. *Leev that uh-LOHN. Stahp that.*	Deja eso.
Don't touch that. It's dirty. *Dohnt tuhch that. Itz DIRT-ee.*	No toques eso. Está sucio.
Don't pick that up. *Dohnt pik that ahp.*	No tomes eso.
Hands off! *Hanz awf!*	¡Saca las manos!
Open the door. *OH-pen th'dor.*	Abre la puerta.
Don't lock the door. *Dohnt lahk th'dor.*	No cierres la puerta con llave.
Don't open the window. *Dohnt OH-pen th'WIN-doh.*	No abras la ventana.
Don't lean out the window. *Dohnt leen aout th'WIN-doh.*	No te apoyes en la ventana.
Close the refrigerator. *Klohz th'ree-FRIJ-er-ei-tr.*	Cierra la nevera.
Don't close the box. *Dohnt klohz th'bahks.*	No cierres la caja.

CONVERSACIÓN

Move the box over there.
Moov th'bahks OH-ver thehr.
Mueve la caja allí. *

Slow down!
Sloh daoun!
¡Despacio!

Don't run! Walk!
Dohnt ruhn! Wawk!
¡No corras! ¡Camina!

Don't hurry. You're going to fall.
Dohnt HUR-ee. Yor GOH-'ng t'fawl.
No te apures. Te vas a caer.

Take your time.
Teik yor tighm.
Tomate tu tiempo.

Hurry!
HUR-ee!
¡Apúrate!

Don't lag behind.
Dohnt lag bee-HIGHND.
No te quedas atrás.

Eat in the kitchen so that you don't stain the rug.
Eet in th'KICH-en soh that yoo dohnt stein th'rug.
Come en la cocina para que no manches la alfombra.

Don't forget to wipe your shoes.
Dohnt for-GET t'wighp yor shooz.
No te olvides de secarte los zapatos.

Put the shoe in its place.
Put th'shoo in itz pleis.
Pon el zapato en su lugar. *

The shoe belongs on the floor.
Th'shoo bee-LAWNGZ ahn th'flor.
El zapato debe estar en el suelo.

Stand there.
Stand thehr.
Párate allí.

Don't write on the wall.
Dohnt right ahn th'wawl.
No escribas en el muro.

Don't touch the stove.
Dohnt tuhch th'stohv.
No toques la estufa.

You're going to burn yourself.
Yor GOH-'ng t'burn yor-SELF.
Te vas a quemar.

Did you burn yourself?
Did yoo burn yor-SELF?
¿Te quemaste?

There's nothing wrong with me.
Thehrz NUTH-'ng rawng with mee.
No me pasa nada.

Don't play with matches.
Dohnt plei with MACH-ez.
No juegues con fósforos. *

Don't go near the stairs.
Dohnt goh neer th'stehrz.
No vayas cerca de la escalera.

Don't cross the street.
Dohnt kraws th'street.
No cruces la calle.

Look both ways before crossing the street.
Luk bohth weiz bee-FOR KRAWS-'ng th'street.
Mira los dos lados antes de cruzar.

Wait for the green light.
Weit for th' green light.
Espera la luz verde. *

From now on, be careful.
Fruhm naou ahn, bee KEHR-ful.
Desde ahora en adelante, ten cuidado.

Hold it/ by the handle/ with two hands/.
Hohld it/ bigh th'HAND-dl/ with too hanz/.
Ten/ lo/ la/ por la manija/ con dos manos/.

Pay attention to what you are doing.
Pei uh-TEN-shuhn t'waht yoo ahr DOO-'ng.
Presta atención a lo que haces.

Don't drop it on the floor.
Dohnt drahp it ahn th'flor.
No lo dejes caer en el suelo.

Don't cut your finger; the knife is sharp.
Dohnt kuht yor FIN-gr; th'nighf iz shahrp.
No te cortes el dedo; el cuchillo está afilado. *

CONVERSACIÓN

Don't grab that. *Dohnt grab that.*	No cojas eso.
...because I said so. *...bee-KAWZ igh sed soh.*	... porque yo lo dije.
... because that's the way it is. *... bee-KAWZ thatz th'wei it iz.*	...porque es así.
Could you please...(bring me the mop)? *Kud yoo pleez...(bring mee th'mahp)?*	¿Por favor, podrias...(traerme la escoba)?
Do you think that...(you could help me prepare lunch)? *Doo yoo think that...(yoo kud help mee pree-PEHR luhnch)?*	¿Crees que... (podrias auydarme a hacer el almuerzo)?
Do you think you can...(carry the dish)? *Doo yoo think yoo kan...(KAR-ee th'dish)?*	¿Crees que puedes...(llevar el plato)?
May I ask you...(why you threw the rock)? *Mei igh ask yoo...(wigh yoo throo th'rahk)?*	¿Puedo preguntarte...(por qué tiraste la piedra)?
Let's try to do it together. *Letz trigh t'doo it tuh-GETH-er.*	Vamos a tratar de hacerlo juntos.
Have your brother/ come upstairs/ come in/. *Hav yor BRUH-ther/ kuhm ahp-STEHRZ/ kuhm in/.*	Que /suba/ entre/ tu hermano.
Tell him to come. *Tel him t'kuhm.*	Dile que venga.
Knock, please. Come in! *Nahk, pleez. Kuhm in!*	Golpea, por favor. ¡Entra!
Go into your room and put on another shirt. *Goh IN-too yor room and put ahn uh-NUTH-er shirt.*	Ve a tu cuarto y ponte otra camisa.

Show me your room.
Shoh mee yor room.

Muestrame tu cuarto.

What are you/ doing / making/?
Waht ahr yoo/ DOO-'ng/ MEIK-'ng/?

¿Qué haces?

Let/ him/ her/ do it.
Let/ him/ her/ doo it.

Que lo haga/ el/ella/.

Sit down. Remain seated.
Sit daoun. Ree-MEIN SEET-ed.

Siéntate. Quédate sentado/a/.

Stand up. Remain standing.
Stand ahp. Ree-MEIN STAND-'ng.

Levántate. Quédate de pie.

Lie down.
Ligh daoun.

Acuéstate.

Rock the baby gently.
Rahk th'BEI-bee JENT-lee.

Mece al bebé suavemente.

Tell me what happened.
Tel mee waht HAP-end.

Dime lo que pasó.

Was it you who did it?
Wuhz it yoo hoo did it?

¿Fuiste tú quien hizo eso?

Did you do it on purpose?
Did yoo doo it ahn PUR-puhs?

¿Lo hiciste a propósito?

Watch your language!
Wahch yor LANG-wij!

¡Cuidado con tu vocabulario!

I want to see/ him/ her/.
Igh wahnt t'see/ him/ her/.

Quiero verlo/ la/.

CONVERSACIÓN

No cursing or swearing! *Noh KURS-'ng or SWEHR-'ng!*	¡No se dicen palabrotas!
I want you to tell me the truth. *Igh wahnt yoo t' tel mee th'trooth.*	Quiero que me digas la verdad.
Speak more/ slowly/ clearly/. *Speek mor/ SLOH-lee/ KLEER-lee/.*	Habla más/ lentamente/ claramente/.
Don't mumble. *Dohnt MUM-bl.*	No hables entre dientes.
Listen carefully. *LIS-en KEHR-fuh-lee.*	Escucha con cuidado.
You are not behaving well today. *Yoo ahr naht bee-HEIV-'ng wel tuh-DEI.*	No te estás portando bien hoy.
Promise me to behave. *PRAH-mis mee t'bee-HEIV.*	Prométeme que te vas a portar bien.
Behave yourself. *Bee-HEIV yor-SELF.*	Pórtate bien.
Do you understand what I'm telling you? *Doo yoo uhn-der-STAND waht ighm TEL-'ng yoo?*	¿Entiendes lo que te digo?
Don't be naughty. *Dohnt bee NAWT-ee.*	No seas malo.
Are you stubborn! *Ahr yoo STUHB-ern!*	¡Qué cabeza dura!
Don't cry. Calm down. *Dohnt krigh. Kahlm daoun.*	No llores. Cálmate.

Don't be nervous.
Dohnt bee NER-vus.

No te pongas nervioso/ a/.

Don't be afraid.
Dohnt bee uh-FREID.

No tengas miedo.

Everything is going to be all right.
EV-ree-thing iz GOH-'ng t'bee awl right.

Todo va a estar bien.

That hurts!
That hurtz!

¡Qué dolor!

Show me where it hurts.
Show mee wehr it hurtz.

Muéstrame donde te duele.

You have some scratches and bruises.
Too hav suhm SKRAT-chez and BROOZ-iz.

Tú tienes algunos rasguños y moratones.

You bumped your nose.
Yoo bumpt yor nohz.

Te golpeaste la nariz.

Rub it with your hand.
Ruhb it with yor hand.

Pásate la manita.

Open your mouth.
OH-pen yor maouth.

Abre la boca.

Don't put the pebble in your mouth.
Dohnt put th'PEH-bl in yor maouth.

No te pongas la piedrita en la boca.

Feel it with your fingers.
Feel it with yor FEEN-gerz.

Siéntelo/ la/ con los dedos.

Don't make faces.
Dohnt meik FEI-sez.

No pongas malas caras.

No whining, moaning.
Noh WIGHN-'ng, MOHN-'ng.

No gimas.

OLDHAM COUNTY PUBLIC LIBRARY

CONVERSACIÓN

It will do you good.
It wil doo yoo gud.

Te hará bien.

Blow your nose.
Bloh yor nohz.

Suénate la nariz.

Breathe through your nose.
Breeth throo yor nohz.

Respira por la nariz.

Don't tell me that.
Dohnt tel mee that.

No me digas eso.

You have an answer for everything.
Yoo hav an AN-ser for EV-ree-thing.

Tienes una respuesta para todo.

Forget your toy for a moment.
For-GET yor toy for uh'MOH-ment.

Olvídate del juguete por un momento.

Use your own toys.
Yooz yor ohn toyz.

Usa tus propios juguetes.

Remember to bring your crayons.
Ree-MEM-ber t'bring yor KREI-ahnz.

Acuérdate de llevar tus crayones. *

Bring me…
Bring mee...

Tráeme...

Come here with me.
Kuhm heer with mee.

Ven acá conmigo.

Immediately.
Ee-MEE-dee-et-lee.

Enseguida.

Go to the bathroom.
Goh t'th'BATH-room.

Ve al baño.

Go first.
Goh first.

Ve primero.

This way. Follow me.
This wei. FAHL-oh mee.
Por acá. Sígueme.

Can (Can't) you do it yourself?
Kan (kant) yoo doo it yor-SELF?
¿(No) puedes hacerlo solo?

Go downstairs and help Grandma.
Goh DAOUN-stehrz and help GRAN(D)-mah.
Ve abajo y ayuda a la abuelita.

Grandfather is hard of hearing.
GRAN(D)-fahth-er iz hahrd uhv'HEER-'ng.
El abuelo no oye bien.

Go/ outside/ inside/ and play.
Goh/ AOUT-sighd/ IN-sighd/ and plei.
Ve /afuera/ adentro/ a jugar.

Come on! Let's go!
Kuhm ahn! Letz goh!
¡Vamonos!

Don't turn off the light.
Dohnt turn awf th'light.
No apagues la luz.

Turn it on again.
Turn it ahn uh-GEHN.
Enciéndela otra vez.

I can't see my way in the dark.
Igh kant see migh wei in th'dahrk.
No puedo ver en la oscuridad.

Press the switch.
Prehs th'switch.
Empuja el botón. *

Turn on the cassette player.
Turn ahn th'kah-SET PLEI-er.
Enciende el tocacintas.

Lower the compact disk player.
LOH-er th'KOM-pakt disk PLEI-er.
Baja el aparato de discos compactos.

Turn off the television.
Turn awf th'TEL-uh-vizh-uhn.
Apaga la televisión. *

CONVERSACIÓN

You may not watch/ this/ that/ program.
Yoo mei naht wahch/ this/ that/ PROH-gram.

No puedes mirar/ este/ ese/ programa.

No TV when you are doing homework.
Noh tee-vee wen yoo ahr DOO-'ng HOHM-wurk.

No hay televisión cuando estás haciendo la tarea.

Hang up the phone.
Hang ahp th'fohn.

Cuelga el teléfono.

Stop playing /computer games/ with the (new) computer.
Stahp PLEI'ng/ kuhm-PYOO-tr geimz/ with th'(nyoo) kuhm-PYOO-tr.

Deja de jugar juegos electrónicos/ con la ordenador (nueva).

It's too late to have friends over.
Itz too leit t'hav frendz OH-ver.

Es demasiado tarde para tener amigos/ amiga/.

That one is not yours.
That wuhn iz naht yorz.

Eso no es tuyo.

That one is yours.
That wuhn iz yorz.

Esa es tuya.

This one is yours.
This wuhn iz yorz.

Este es tuyo.

This one is yours.
This wuhn iz yorz.

Esta es tuya.

There is yours.
Thehr iz yorz.

Allí está/ el tuyo/ la tuya/.

Your book is overdue.
Yor buk iz OH-ver-doo.

El plazo de devolución de tu libro está vencido.

Return your book (to the library).
Ree-TURN yor buk (t'th'LIGH-brehr-ee).

Devuelve el libro (a la biblioteca).

You have/ soccer practice/ music lessons/ today.
Yoo hav/ SAHK-er PRAK-tis/ MYOO-zik LEHS-ens/ tuh-DEI.

Tienes/ práctica de fútbol/ lecciones de música/ hoy.

Fasten your seat belt.
FAS-en yor seet belt.

Abrochate el cinturón de seguridad.

Who's been running up the phone bill?
Hooz ben RUHN-'ng ahp th'fohn bil?

¿Quién está subiendo la cuenta telefónica?

You have to feed the/ dog/ cat/.
Yoo hav t'feed th'/dawg/ kat/.

Tienes que dar de comer al / perro/ gato/.

It's your turn to/ take the dog for a walk/ take out the garbage/.
Itz yor turn t'/ teik th'dawg for uh'wawk/ teik aout th'GAHR-bij/.

Te toca a tí/ sacar el perro a pasear/ sacar la basura/.

Takc off the head set!
Teik awf th'hed set!

¡Quitate los audífonos! *

Be home on time
Bee hohm ahn tighm.

Estate en casa a tiempo.

Don't be late.
Dohnt bee leit.

No llegues tarde.

Complaints not accepted here!
Kuhm-pleints naht ak-SEPT-ed heer!

¡No presentes quejas aquí!

It's time you were leaving.
Itz tighm yoo wuhr LEEV-'ng.

Es hora de que te vayas.

Be a good boy.
Bee uh'gud boy.

Sé bueno.

Be a good girl.
Bee uh'gud girl.

Sé buena.

HELPING *at* HOME	AYUDANDO *en* CASA

Help me set the table.
Help mee set th'TEI-bl.

Ayúdame a poner la mesa.

You can put on the tablecloth and napkins.
Yoo kan put ahn th'TEI-bl-klawth and NAP-kinz.

Puedes poner el mantel y las servilletas.

/Set/ Clear/ the table, please.
/Set/ Kleer/ th'TEI-bl, pleez.

/Pon/ Levanta/ la mesa, por favor.

Help me/ wash/ dry/ the dishes.
Help mee/ wahsh/ drigh/ th'DISH-ez.

Ayúdame a/ lavar/ secar/ los platos.

Help me/ make the bed/ clean the house/ do the wash/.
Help mee/ meik th'bed/ kleen th'haous/ doo th'wahsh/.

Ayúdame a/ hacer la cama/ limpiar la casa/ lavar la ropa/.

Did you make your bed?
Did yoo meik yor bed?

¿Hiciste la cama?

Why not?
Wigh naht?

¿Por qué no?

You're supposed to make your bed.
Yor suh-POHZD t'meik yor bed.

Tú tienes que hacer tu cama.

You make work!
Yoo meik mee wurk!

¡Me haces trabajar!

Mommy is sweeping the floor.
MAH-mee iz SWEEP-'ng th'flor.

Mami está barriendo el suelo.

Daddy vacuums the rug.
DAD-ee VAK-kyooms th'rug.

Papi está pasando la aspiradora. *

The vacuum makes a strange noise.
Th'VAK-kyoom meiks uh'stranj noyz.

La aspiradora hace un ruido extraño.

What dust! Let's dust.
Waht duhst! Letz duhst.

¡Qué polvo! Vamos a quitar el polvo.

Take the dust cloth in your hand, and rub. Like this.
Teik th'duhst klawth in yor hand, and ruhb. Lighk this.

Toma el trapo con tu mano y friega. Así.

I'm sewing a skirt for the baby.
Ighm SOH-'ng uh'skirt for th'BEI-bee.

Estoy cosiendo una falda para la bebé.

Help father cook dinner.
Help FAH-ther kuk DIN-er.

Ayúdale a tu padre a hacer la cena.

Mother is baking a cake.
MUH-ther iz BEIK-'ng uh'keik.

Mamá está haciendo una tarta. *

Do you want to help me bake cookies?
Doo yoo wahnt t'help mee beik KUK-eez?

¿Me quieres ayudar a hacer galletitas?

Pour in the flour.
Por in th'FLAOU-er.

Echa la harina.

I'll add the sugar.
Ighl ad th'SHUG-er.

Agrego el azúcar.

I'm mixing the sugar and the butter.
Ighm MIKS-'ng th'SHUG-er and th'BUH-tr.

Mezclo el azúcar y la mantequilla. *

Do we need baking powder?
Doo wee need BEIK-'ng PAOU-der?

¿Necesitamos la levadura?

I'm beating the eggs.
Ighm BEET-'ng th'eigz.

Estoy revolviendo los huevos.

Roll the dough.
Rohl th'doh.

Estira la masa. *

We bake them in the oven.
Wee beik them in th'UHV-en.

Los cocemos en el horno.

Set the clock for one-half hour.
Set th'klahk for wuhn-haf aour.

Pon el reloj para media hora.

The cookies are done.
Th'KUK-eez ahr duhn.

Las galletitas están hechas.

You cannot help me iron.
Yoo KAN-naht help mee IGH-uhrn.

No me puedes ayudar a planchar.

You can help me/ sort/ fold/ the laundry.
Yoo kan help mee/ sawrt/ fohld/ th'LAWN-dree.

Me puedes ayudar a / separar/ doblar/ la ropa.

After cleaning, we can read a story.
AF-tr KLEEN-'ng, wee kan reed uh'STOR-ee.

Después de limpiar, podemos leer un cuento.

Before playing, you must straighten your room.
Bee-FOR PLEI-'ng, yoo muhst STREIT-en yor room.

Antes de jugar, tienes que arreglar tu cuarto.

Put all the pots back in the cupboard.
Put awl th'pahtz bak in th'KUB-bord.

Vuelvc a poner todas las ollas en la alacena.

Can you help me wrap the present?
Kan yoo help mee rap th'PREH-zent?

¿Puedes ayudarme a envolver el regalo?

There are so many weeds!
Thehr ahr soh MEN-ee weedz!

¡Qué maleza hay!

We need to weed the garden so that the plants will grow.
Wee need t'weed th'GAHR-den soh that th'plantz wil groh.

Tenemos que quitar la maleza para que crezcan las plantas.

Plant the seeds in a row.
Plant th'seedz in uh'roh.

Planta las semillas en una fila.

Help me cut the lawn.
Help mee kuht th'lawn.

Ayúdame a cortar el césped.

Will you help me water the garden?
Will yoo help mee WAW-tr th'GAHR-den?

¿Me ayudarás a regar el jardín?

Don't strain yourself.
Dohnt strein YOR-self.

No te esfucrces demasiado.

Don't dig too much.
Dohnt dig too muhch.

No caves tanto.

Dig a little hole here.
Dig uh'LIT-le hohl heer.

Cava un hueco pequeño aquí.

Be careful of the caterpillars.
Bee KEHR-fl uhv'th'KAT-er-pil-erz.

Ten cuidado con las orugas. *

AYUDANDO *en* CASA

Can you rake the leaves? *Kan yoo reik th'leevz?*	¿Puedes rastrillar las hojas?
Throw the leaves into the garbage pail. *Throh th'leevz IN-too th'GAHR-bij peil.*	Echa las hojas en el cesto de la basura.
You cannot prune the trees. *Yoo KAN-naht proon th'treez.*	No puedes podar los árboles.
It is too dangerous. *It iz too DEIN-jer-us.*	Es demasiado peligroso.
Instead of pruning, you can help me make a wagon. *In-STED uhv'PROON-'ng, yoo kan help mee meik uh'WAG-un.*	En vez de podar, puedes ayudarme a hacer un carretilla.
Can you sand this piece of wood? *Kan yoo sand this pees uhv'wud?*	¿Puedes lijar este pedazo de madera?
Saw this board in two. *Saw this bord in too.*	Serrucha este tablero en dos partes. *
Give me the screwdriver. *Giv mee th'SKROO-drigh-vr.*	Dame el destornillador.
Hammer this nail. *HAM-er this neil.*	Martilla este clavo. *
I have to work on our airplane. *Igh hav t'wurk ahn aour EHR-plein.*	Tengo que trabajar en nuestro avión.
Do you want to watch? *Doo yoo wahnt t'wahch?*	¿Quieres mirar?
Our boat needs painting. *Aour boht needz PEINT-'ng.*	Hay que pintar nuestro barco. *

We have to work on the car.
Wee hav t' wurk ahn th'kahr.

Tenemos que trabajar en el coche.

/Wash/ Vacuum/ the car.
/Wahsh/ VAK-yoom/ th'kahr.

/Lava / Pasa la aspiradora/
el coche.

Sweep the sidewalk.
Sweep th'SIGHD-wawk.

Barre la acera.

We need to shovel the snow.
Wee need t'SHUV-el th'snoh.

Necesitamos quitar la nieve.

Help me connect the computer to the monitor.
Help mee kuh-NEKT th'kuhm-PYOO-tr t'th'MAHN-ih-tr.

Ayúdame conectar la computadora
al monitor.

Here is your allowance.
Heer is yor ah-LAOU-ens.

Aquí está tu paga.

SCHOOL *at* HOME	CLASES *en* CASA

The school bus just went by!
Th'skool buhs juhst went bigh!

¡El autobús escolar acaba de pasar!

It's time for us to start, too.
Itz tighm for uhs t'stahrt, too.

Tambien es hora de empezar.

What is today's date?
Waht iz tuh-DEIZ deit?

¿Cuál es la fecha de hoy?

Today is October 14.
Tuh-DEI iz ahk-TOH-br for-TEENTH.

Hoy es el 14 de octubre.

Where did we leave off yesterday?
Wehr did wee leev awf YEHS-tr-dei?

¿Dónde quedamos ayer?

We will need scotch tape,
a stapler, scissors, and paper.
Wee wil need skahch teip,
uh'STEIP-lr, SIHZ-erz, and PAE-per.

Necesitaremos cinta Scotch, una grapadora, tijeras, y papel. *

There/ are no staples/ is no glue/.
Thehr/ ahr noh STEIP-ulz/ iz noh gloo/.

No hay/ grapas/ goma/.

There's:
Thehrz:

Hay:

the fish project,
th'fish PRAH-jekt,

el proyecto de los peces,

the boat project,
th'boht PRAH-jekt,

el proyecto del barco,

the map project,
th'map PRAH-jekt,

el proyecto del mapa,

to do.
t'doo.

para hacer.

I need more time to finish the project.
Igh need mor tighm t'FIN-ish th'PRAH-jekt.

Necesito más tiempo para terminar el proyecto.

Would you help me with my homework?
Wud yoo help mee with migh HOHM-wurk?

¿Me ayudarías con la tarea?

I don't understand it.
Igh dohnt uhn-der-STAND it.

No la entiendo.

By when do I have to finish the report?
Bigh wen doo igh hav t'FIN-ish th'ree-PORT?

¿Para cuándo tengo que terminar el informe?

I don't know for sure.
I don't know for shuur.

No sé bien.

Check the bulletin board.
Chek th'BUL-eh-tin bord.

Chequee el tablero.

Do you have something to do?
Doo yoo hav SUHM-thing t'doo?

¿Tienes algo que hacer?

I can help you with that.
Igh kan help yoo with that.

En eso puedo aconsejarte.

Do we have to study science?
Doo wee hav t'STUH-dee SIGH-ens?

¿Tenemos que estudiar ciencias?

I'm getting tired of /studying/ working/.
Ighm GET-'ng TIGHR-ed uhv'/ STUHD-ee-'ng/ WURK-'ng/.

Me canso de /estudiar/ trabajar/.

Here are my pen and ink drawings.
Heer ahr migh pen and ink DRAW-'ngz.

Aquí está mi dibujo a la pluma.

Do your reading while I work with your brother.
Doo yor REED-'ng wighl igh wurk with yor BRUTH-er.

Lee para ti mientras que yo trabajo con tu hermano.

Keep reading. Add the numbers.
Keep REED-'ng. Ad th'NUHM-berz.

Sigue leyendo. Suma los números.

No wonder you like to read.
Noh WUHN-dr yoo lighk t'reed.

Con razón te gusta leer.

Do you want to ask a question?
Doo yoo wahnt t'ask uh'KWESH-'tn?

¿Quieres hacer una pregunta?

Show your sister how to do her math problems.
Shoh yor SIS-tr haou t'doo her math PRAH-blemz.

Muestra a tu hermana como hacer sus problemas de matemáticas. *

Teach yourself.
Teech yor-SELF.

Enseñate.

Mom, the hole punch is stuck.
Mahm, th'hohl punch iz stuhk.

Mami, el perforador está atascado.

Can we take a break for a while?
Kan wee teik uh'breik for uh'wighl?

¿Podemos descansar un rato?

Let's get a snack from the kitchen.
Letz get uh'snak fruhm th'KIT-chen.

Vamos a la cocina a buscar la merienda.

When we come back:
Wen wee kuhm bak:

Cuando volvamos:

we'll read,
weel reed,

leeremos,

we can get on the Internet,
wee kan get ahn th'IN-ter-net,

podemos conectarle al internet,

we'll send e-mail,
weel send ee-meil,

enviaremos correo electrónico,

we'll bake cookies for Uncle Peter,
weel beik KUK-eez for UN-kl PEE-tr,

haremos galletitas para el tío Pedro,

we'll paint a picture for daddy.
weel peint uh'PIK-chur for DAD-ee.

pintaremos un dibujo para papi.

Let's exercise.
Letz EKS-er-sighz.

Hagamos ejercicios físicos.

We'll work in the garden.
Weel wurk in th'GAHR-den.

Trabajaremos en el jardín. *

Look at the screen (of the computer).
Luk at th'skreen (uv'th'kuhm-PYOO-tr).

Fíjate en la pantalla.

The /computer/ keyboard/ printer/ is not working well.
Th'/kuhm-PYOO-tr/ KEE-bord/ PRIN-tr/ iz naht WURK-'ng wel.

/El ordenador/ el teclado/ la impresora/ no funciona bien.

When is the computer going to be fixed?
Wen iz th'kuhm-PYOO-tr GOH-'ng t'bee fixt?

¿Cuándo se va a arreglar el ordenador? *

Could we have connected the cables incorrectly?
Kud wee hav kuh-NEKT-ed th'KEI-blz in-kuh-REKT-lee?

¿Habremos conectado mal los cables?

I want to/ open/ close/ save/ a file.
Igh wahnt t'/OH-pen/ klohz/ seiv/ uh'fighl.

Quiero/ abrir / cerrar/ guardar/ un archivo.

The instructions that came with the computer are difficult.
Th'in-STRUHK-shuhnz that keim with th' kuhm-PYOO-tr ahr DIF-ih-kult.

Las instrucciones que vinieron con el ordenador son dificiles.

I can't remember my password.
Igh kant ree-MEM-br migh PAS-wurd.

No recuerdo mi contraseña.

I'm glad we don't have to take an exam.
Ighm glad wee dohnt hav t'teik an eks-AM.

Me alegro de que no tengamos que tomar un examen.

We have to study.
Wee hav t'STUH-dee.

Tenemos que estudiar.

I have three pages left to read in this book.
Igh hav three PEI-jez left t'reed in this buk.

A mí me faltan tres páginas para terminar de leer este libro.

I'll leave you to your work.
Ighl leev yoo t'yor wurk.

Te dejo con tus tareas.

I need extra time for my music.
Igh need EKS-truh tighm for migh MYOO-zik.

Necesito más tiempo para mi música. *

Where is my newspaper clipping?
Wehr iz migh NYOOZ-pei-per KLIP'ng?

¿Dónde está mi recorte?

Can I skip history?
Kan igh skip HIST-ree?

¿Puedo omitir la historia?

My colored pencils are missing.
Migh KUL-urd PEN-silz ahr MIS-'ng.

Mis lápices de colores están perdidos. *

Where could my pencils be?
Wehr kud migh PEN-silz bee?

¿Dónde estarán mis lápices? *

Could I have left them in the car?
Kud igh hav left them in th'kahr?

¿Los habré dejado en el coche?

Has anyone seen them?
Haz EN-ee-wuhn seen them?

¿Los ha visto alguien?

I want to draw lines with them.
Igh wahnt t'draw lighnz with them.

Quiero subrayar con ellos.

Mom, where are the/ pipe cleaners/ toothpicks/?
Mahm, wehr ahr th'/ pighp KLEEN-erz/ TOOTH-piks/?

¿Mami, dónde están los /limpiapipas/ palillos/?

You did a lot of work!
Yoo did uh'laht uhv'wurk!

¡Tú trabajaste mucho!

You deserve a treat.
Yoo dee-ZERV uh'treet.

Te mereces un premio. *

PRAISE	ALABANZA
What a beautiful voice! *Waht uh'BYOO-tih-ful voys!*	¡Qué linda voz!
You/ walk/ draw/ speak/ sing/ dance/ well. *Yoo/ wawk/ draw/ speek/ sing/ dans/ wel.*	Caminas/ dibujas/ hablas/ cantas/ bailas bien.
How well you/ write/ swim/ play/! *Haou wel yoo/ right/ swim/ plei/!*	¡Qué bien /escribes/ nadas / juegas/!
You're wonderful! *Yor WUHN-dr-ful!*	¡Eres maravilloso/ a/!
You're brilliant! *Yor BRIL-yent!*	¡Eres brillante!
How sweet you are! *Haou sweet yoo ahr!*	¡Qué dulce eres!

How/ pretty/ handsome/ you are!
Haou/ PRIH-tee/ HAND-suhm/ yoo ahr!

¡Qué/ linda/ buen mozo/ eres!

How clever you are!
Haou KLEV-er yoo ahr!

¡Qué listo /a/ eres!

How cute you are.
Haou kyoot yoo ahr.

Qué mono/a/ eres.

This dress suits you well.
This dres sootz yoo wel.

Este vestido te queda bien.

What pretty eyes you have!
Waht PRIH-tee ighz yoo hav!

¡Qué ojos más bonitos tienes!

I love/ your eyes/ your hands/.
Igh luhv/ yor ighz/ yor hanz/.

Me encantan tus /ojos /manos/.

I love your tummy.
Igh luhv yor TUM-ee.

Me encanta tu pancita.

What pretty curls!
Waht PRIH-tee kurlz!

¡Qué lindos rizos!

What a good girl!
Waht uh'gud gurl!

¡Qué buena chica! *

What a good boy!
Waht uh'gud boy!

¡Qué buen chico! *

How nice you are!
Haou nighs yoo ahr!

¡Qué simpatico/a/ eres!

That's nice of you.
Thatz nighs uhv'yoo.

Qué agradable.

You are in good spirits.
Yoo ahr in gud SPIR-itz.

Estás de buen humor.

I like you. I love you. *Igh lighk yoo. Igh luhv yoo.*	Me gustas. Te quiero.
Well done! *Wel duhn!*	¡Bien hecho!
You hit the mark! *Yoo hit th'mahrk!*	¡Diste en el blanco!
That's correct. *That's kuh-REKT.*	Es correcto.
I like the way you play quietly by yourself. *Igh lighk th'wei yoo plei KWIGH-et-lee bigh yor-SELF.*	Me gusta como juegas calladamente y solito/a.
You were nice to give me the towel. *Yoo wuhr nighs t'giv mee th'taoul.*	Fuiste muy amable en darme la toalla.
Keep trying. Don't give up. *Keep TRIGH-'ng. Dohnt giv ahp.*	Sigue tratando. No te des por vencido.
What a magnificent idea! *Waht uh'mag-NIF-ih-sent igh-DEE-uh!*	¡Qué idea tan magnífica!
You're getting better and better. *Yor GET-'ng BET-er and BET-er.*	Estás mejorando más y más.
I certainly liked your help. *Igh SUR-ten-lee lighkd yor help.*	Ciertamente me ha gustado tu ayuda.
You cleaned your room well. *Yoo kleend yor room wel.*	Limpiaste bien tu cuarto.
You were patient while I was talking on the phone. *Yoo wuhr PEI-shent wighl igh wuhz TAWK-'ng ahn th'fohn.*	Fuiste paciente mientras hablaba por teléfono. *

No todo lo que brilla es oro. All that glitters is not gold.

SHOPPING COMPRAS

Do you want to go shopping? *Doo yoo wahnt t'goh SHAHP-'ng?*	¿Quieres ir de compras?
I'm going to the market. *Ighm GOH-'ng t'th'MAHR-ket.*	Voy al mercado.
I need to buy... *Igh need t'bigh...*	Necesito comprar...
I need to return... (an item) *Igh need t'ree-TURN...*	Tengo que devolver...
There's a sale. *Thehrz uh'seil.*	Hay rebajas.
What bargains! *Waht BAHR-ghenz!*	¡Qué gangas!

What will you buy with your dollar?
Waht wil yoo bigh with yor DAHL-er?

¿Qué vas a comprar con tu dólar? *

Let's take the/elevator/ escalator/.
Letz teik th'/EL-uh-vei-tr/ ES-kuh-lei-tr/.

Vamos a coger/el ascensor/ la escalera mecánica/.

You need new clothes.
Yoo need nyoo klohz.

Necesitas ropa nueva.

We cannot spend too much money.
Wee KAN-naht spend too muhch MUHN-ee.

No podemos gastar demasiado dinero.

We cannot buy that.
Wee KAN-naht bigh that.

No podemos comprar eso.

That's too expensive.
Thats too eks-PEN-siv.

Es demasiado caro/ a/.

Perhaps something cheaper.
Per-HAPS SUHM-thing CHEEP-er.

Quizás algo más barato.

I'm short of money.
Ighm short uhv'MUHN-ee.

Me falta dinero.

The sales clerk is over there.
Th'seilz klerk iz OH-ver thehr.

/El vendedor/ la vendedora/ está allí.

How much does it cost?
Haou muhch duhz it kawst?

¿Cuánto cuesta?

Should we buy it?
Shud wee bigh it?

¿Lo/ La/ compramos?

What size is this coat?
Waht sighz iz this koht?

¿Qué talla tiene este abrigo?

Let me see that.
Let mee see that.

Déjame ver eso.

Try it on.
Trigh it ahn.

Pruébatelo/ la/.

It looks good on you.
It luks gud ahn yoo.

Te queda bien.

I'll get in line (to pay).
Ighl get in lighn (t'pei).

Yo me pongo en la cola (para pagar).

Count your change.
Kaount yor cheinj.

Cuenta el cambio.

Would you like to go with me:
Wud yoo lighk t'goh with mee:

¿Te gustaría ir conmigo:

to the bakery,
t'th'BEIK-ree,

a la panadería,

to the grocery store,
t'th'GROH-sree stor,

al mercado,

to the laundromat,
t'th LAWN-druh-mat,

a la lavandería,

to the supermarket,
t'th SOO-per-mahr-ket,

al supermercado,

to the department store,
t'th dee-PAHRT-ment stor,

al almacén,

to the drug store,
t'th'druhg stor,

a la farmacia,

to the butcher shop,
t'th' BUT-cher shahp,

a la carnicería,

to the toy store,
t'th' toy stor,

a la juguetería,

to the bank, *t'th'bank,*	al banco,
to the library, *t'th LIGH-brehr-ee,*	a la biblioteca,
to the shoe store, *t'th shoo stor,*	a la zapatería,
to the shoemaker? *t'th SHOO-meik-er?*	al zapatero?
I'm going to park the car. *Ighm GOH-'ng t'pahrk th'kahr.*	Yo voy a aparcar.
Don't walk behind me. *Dohnt wawk bee-HIGHND mee.*	No caminas atrás.
Would you want to go with me: *Wud yoo lighk t'goh with mee:*	¿Te gustaría ir conmigo:
to the lumber yard, *t'th'LUHM-ber yahrd,*	al depósito de madera,
to the hardware store, *t'th'HAHRD-wehr stor,*	a la ferretería,
to the nursery, *t'th'NURS-ree,*	a la jardinería,
to the gas station, *t'th'gas STEI-shuhn,*	a la estación de gasolina,
to the airport, *t'th EHR-port,*	al aeropuerto,
to the marina, *t'th mah-REEN-ah,*	a la marina,

to the pet shop?
t'th'pet shahp?

al la tienda de animales? *

This is too:
This iz too:

Es demasido:

tight,
tight,

apretado/ a/,

loose,
loos,

suelto/ a/,

large,
lahrj,

grande,

small.
smawl.

pequeño/a/.

We need to buy groceries.
Wee need t'bigh GROH-sreez.

Necesitamos comprar comida.

You can sit in the (shopping) cart.
Yoo kan sit in th'(SHAHP-'ng) kahrt.

Puedes sentarte en el carrito (del supermercado).

Stay in the (shopping) cart.
Stei in th'(SHAHP-'ng) kahrt.

Quédate en el carrito. *

Put your feet through the openings.
Put yor feet throo th'OH-pen-'ngz.

Mete los pies en las aberturas.

Don't touch that.
Dohnt tuhch that.

No toques eso.

Do you need to go to to the bathroom?
Doo yoo need t'goh t'th'BATH-room?

¿Necesitas ir al baño?

Let's go to the toy department.
Letz goh t'th' toy dee-PAHRT-ment.

Vamos a la sección de juguetes.

FUN !	¡DIVERSIÓN !

You can:
Yoo kan:

Tú puedes:

play in the yard,
plei in th'yahrd,

jugar en el patio,

go to the playground,
goh t'th' PLEI-graound,

ir al patio del recreo,

go to the (soccer, baseball) field,
goh t'th'(SAHK-er, BEIS-bahl) feeld,

ir al campo (de fútbol, de béisbol),

go to your friend's house.
goh t'yor frendz haous.

ir a la casa de /tu amigo/ tu amiga/.

Are you satisfied with playing at home?
Ahr yoo SAT-is-fighd with PLEI-'ng at hohm?

¿Te contentas con jugar en casa?

Ask them if they want to play:
Ask them if thei wahnt t'plei:

Pregúntales si quieren jugar:

doctor and nurse,
DAHK-ter and nurs,

al médico y a la enfermera, *

store,
stor,

a la tienda,

mother and father,
MUHTH-er and FAHTH-er,

a mamá y papá,

dolls,
dahlz,

a las muñecas,

hopscotch,
HAHP-skahch,

a rayuela,

cowboys and indians,
KAOU-boyz and IN-dyehnz,

a vaqueros e indios,

hide and seek,
highd and seek,

al escondite,

computer games.
kuhm-PYOO-ter geimz.

a los juegos electrónicos.

(ANIMALS) ANIMALES

My trunk is long; I'm large;
and I walk like this. What animal am I?
Migh truhnk iz lawng; Ighm lahrj;
and igh wawk lighk this. Waht AN-i-mul am igh?

Mi trompa es larga; soy grande;
y camino así. ¿Qué animal soy? *

I have two humps; and I lie down like this.
What animal am I?
Igh hav too humps; and igh ligh daoun lighk this.
Waht AN-i-mul am igh?

Tengo dos jorobas; y me acuesto así.
¿Qué animal soy? *

I bark and growl. What animal am I?
Igh bahrk and graoul. Waht AN-i-mul am igh?

Ladro y gruño. ¿Qué animal soy?

Let's pretend that we're kangaroos.
Let's hop.
Letz pree-TEND that weer KANG-guh-rooz.
Letz hahp.

Pretendamos que somos canguros.
Brinquemos. *

Let's pretend we're roosters. Let's crow.
Cock-a-doodle-do!
Letz pree-TEND weer ROOS-terz. Letz
kroh. KAHK-uh-doo-dl-DOO!

Pretendamos que somos gallos. Vamos
a cacarear. ¡Qui-qui-ri-quí! *

(AUTOMOBILES)

AUTOMÓBILES

The car doesn't start.
Th'kahr DUHZ'nt start.

El coche no se pone en marcha. *

The car is out of gas.
Th'kahr iz aout uhv'gas.

Se acabó la gasolina del coche.

It doesn't go anymore.
It DUHZ'nt goh EN-ee-mor.

No va más.

Why doesn't the car go?
Wigh DUHZ'nt th'kahr goh?

¿Por qué no marcha el coche?

Push the car.
Push th'kahr.

Empuja el coche.

Fill'er up.
Fil-er ahp.

Llénelo.

Check the oil, water and battery.
Chek th'oyl, WAW-tr and BAT-er-ee.

Chequee el aceite, el agua y la batería.

How many cylinders does it have?
Haou MEN-ee SIL-en-derz duhz it hav?

¿Cuántos cilindros tiene?

Drive the car into the garage.
Drighv th'kahr IN-too th'gah-RAHJ.

Maneja el coche al garage.

Step on it!
Step ahn it!

¡Date prisa!

My favorite car is a.............
Migh FEIV-ur-it kahr iz uh.......

Mi coche favorito es...

(AIRPLANES) AVIONES

Pilot to control tower.
PIGH-lut t'kon-TROHL TAOU-er.

Piloto a la torre de control.

Fasten your seat belts.
FAS-en yor seet beltz.

Abróchense los cinturones.

I'm taxiing.
Ighm TAK-see-'ng.

Estoy carreteando.

I'm taking off.
Ighm TEIK-'ng awf.

Estoy despegando.

May we land?
Mei wee land?

¿Podemos aterrizar?

We're out of gas!
Weer aout uhv'gas!

¡Se acabó la gasolina del avión!

On which runway may we land?
Ahn wich RUHN-wei mei wee land?

¿En que vía podemos aterrizar?

I worked three weeks on my airplane.
Igh wurkt three weeks ahn migh EHR-plein.

Yo trabajé tres semanas haciendo mi avión. *

(BOATS) BARCOS

All aboard!
Awl uh-BORD!

¡Abordo!

We're sailing to Mexico. *Weer SEIL-'ng t'MEKS-ee-koh.*	Navegamos para México.
The boat is sinking! *Th'boht iz SINK-'ng!*	¡El barco se está hundiendo!
Man overboard! *Man OH-ver-bord!*	¡Hombre al mar!
Abandon ship! *Uh-BAND-uhn ship!*	¡Abandonen el barco!
Lower the life boats! *LOH-er th'lighf bohtz!*	¡Bajen las lanchas salvavidas! *
We're docking. *Weer DAHK-'ng.*	Entramos en el muelle. *

(BASEBALL) **BÉISBOL**

It's your turn. *Itz yor turn.*	Te toca a tí.
/Catch/ throw/ the ball. */Kach/ throh/ th'bawl.*	/Coge/ tira/ la pelota.
Hold the bat behind you. *Hohld th'bat bee-highnd yoo.*	Agarra el bate detrás de tí.
Keep your eye on the ball. *Keep yor igh ahn th'bawl.*	Mantén el ojo en la pelota.
Swing! (the bat) *Swing! (th'bat)*	¡Batea! (el bate) *
Hit the ball! *Hit th'bawl!*	¡Pega la pelota!
You missed! (hitting or catching a ball) *Yoo mist! (th'bawl)*	¡Perdiste! (la pelota)

You hit the ball very well.
Yoo hit th'bawl VER-ee wel.

Golpeas la pelota muy bien.

(CAMPING) **CAMPING**

I'm going camping.
Ighm GOH-'ng KAMP-'ng.

Voy de camping. *

We need a new tent.
Wee need uh'nyoo tent.

Necesitamos una carpa nueva.

This one has holes in it.
This wuhn haz hohlz in it.

Ésta (f) tiene agujeros.

I am happy that we still have our camper.
Igh am HAH-pee that wee still hav aour KAMP-'er.

Me alegro de que todavía tengamos el camper.

Let's pitch the tent here.
Letz pitch th'tent heer.

Armemos la carpa aquí.

I want a campsite right on the lake.
Igh wahnt uh'KAMP-sight right ahn th'leik.

Quiero un camping al lado del lago.

Set up the stove.
Set ahp th'stohv.

Monta el hornillo.

(BICYCLING) **CICLISMO**

Put your foot on the pedal.
Put yor foot ahn th'PED-ul.

Pon el pie en el pedal.

Don't pedal so fast!
Dohnt PED-ul soh fast!

¡No pedalees tan rápido!

Try to keep your balance.
Trigh t'keep yor BAL-ens.

Trata de mantener el equilibrio.

I've got hold of you.
Ighv gaht hold uhv'yoo.

Yo te estoy agarrando.

Let me try.
Let mee trigh.

Déjame intentar.

Hold on to the handlebars.
Hohld ahn t'th'HAND-le-bahrz.

Agarra el manubrio.

Steer/ straight ahead/ straight/ left/.
Steer/ streit uh-HED/ streit/ left/.

Maneja/ todo derecho/ a la derecha/ a la izquierda/. *

Keep pedaling.
Keep PED-ul-'ng.

Sigue pedaleando.

You're riding your bicycle very well.
Yor RIGHD-'ng yor BIGH-sih-kl VER-ee wel.

Montas muy bien en bicicleta.

Ring the bell.
Ring th'bel.

Toca el timbre.

Don't ride your bicycle in the street.
There's too much traffic.
Dohnt righd yor BIGH-sih-kl in th'street.
Thehrz too muhch TRAF-ik.

No andes en bicicleta en la calle.
Hay demasiado tráfico.

You're going too fast.
Yor GOH-'ng too fast.

Vas demasiado rápido.

Put on the brakes!
Put ahn th'breiks!

¡Frena!

You need to put on your helmet.
Yoo need t'put ahn yor HEL-met.

Tienes que ponerte el casco.

Did you hurt yourself?
Did yoo hurt yor-SELF?

¿Te lastimaste?

(COMPUTERS) **COMPUTADORES**

Do you want to play a computer game?
Doo yoo wahnt t'plei uh'kuhm-PYOO-ter geim?
¿Quieres jugar juegos electrónicos? *

Let's print the file.
Letz print th'fighl.
Vamos a imprimir el archivo.

There's a computer error.
Thehrz uh'kuhm-PYOO-ter EHR-er.
Hay un error electrónico.

Don't erase the file!
Dohnt ee-REIS th'fighl!
¡No borres el archivo!

I want to use the scanner.
Igh wahnt t'yooz th'SKAN-er.
Quiero usar el explorador.

(BODY PARTS) **EL CUERPO**

With what:
With waht:
¿Con qué:

do you run, (legs)
doo yoo ruhn, (legz)
corres, (las piernas)

do you speak, (mouth)
doo yoo speek, (maouth)
hablas, (la boca)

do you see, (eyes)
doo yoo see, (ighz)
ves, (los ojos)

do you stand on tiptoe? (toes)
doo yoo stand ahn TIP-toh? (tohz)
te paras en puntas? (los dedos del pie)

(SOCCER) **EL FÚTBOL**

Don't touch the ball with your hands.
Dohnt tuhch th'bawl with yor handz.
No toques la pelota con las manos. *

Kick the ball into the goal.
Kik th'bawl IN-too th'gohl.

Patea la pelota y mete un gol.

What a great save!
Waht uh'greit seiv!

¡Qué salvada!

Look at your footwork!
Luk at yor FUT-wurk!

¡Mira cómo gambeteas!

What a/ goal/ foul/ penalty kick/!
Waht uh/gohl/ faoul/ PEN-ul-tee kik/!

¡Qué /golazo/ foul/ penal/!

This game is close.
This geim iz klohs.

Este partido está reñido.

Pass/ the ball/ to me.
Pas/ th'bawl/ t'mee.

Pasame/ la pelota.

That was a good pass!
That wuhz uh'gud pas!

¡Qué buen pase!

You have scored a goal!
Yoo hav skord uh'gohl!

¡Has marcado un gol!

The referee is blowing his whistle.
Th'REF-er-ee iz BLOH'ng hiz HWIS-ul.

El árbitro toca el silbato.

(BACKYARD)

JARDÍN TRASERO

Go/ outside/ inside/ to play.
Goh/ AOUT-sighd/ IN-sighd/ t'plei.

Anda a jugar/ afuera /adentro/.

Play in/ the yard/ the sandbox/.
Plei in/ th'yahrd/ th'SAND-bahks/.

Juega en/ el jardín/ la caja de arena/.

Do you want to blow bubbles?
Doo yoo wahnt t'bloh BUHB-lz?

¿Quieres hacer burbujas? *

Don't play in the dirt.
Dohnt plei in th'dirt.

No juegues en la tierra.

Don't pick the flowers.
Dohnt pik th'FLAOU-erz.

No recojas las flores.

You can swim in the pool if I am with you.
Yoo kan swim in th'pool if igh am with yoo.

Puedes nadar en la piscina si estoy contigo.

Jump off the diving board as I showed you.
Jump awf th'DIGHV-'ng bord az igh shohd yoo.

Salta del trampolín como te enseñé.

Be careful when you climb trees.
Bee KEHR-ful wen yoo klighm treez.

Ten cuidado cuando te trepes en los árboles.

Both of you can sit in the wagon.
Bohth uhv'yoo kan sit in th'WAG-un.

Los dos pueden sentarse en la carretilla.

There's room enough for two.
Thehrz room ih-NUHF for too.

Hay lugar para dos.

Don't leave the yard.
Dohnt leev th'yahrd.

No salgas del patio.

(BOARD GAMES) JUEGOS de MESA

Do you want to play/ checkers/ chess/?
Doo yoo wahnt t'plei/ CHEHK-erz/ chehs/?

¿Quieres jugar/ a las damas/ una partida de ajedrez/ juego de mesa/? *

Whose move is it?
Hooz moov iz it?

¿Quién va?

Whose turn is it?
Hooz turn iz it?

¿A quién le toca?

It's Joseph's turn.
Itz JOHS-evs turn.

Le toca a José.

It's/ your/ my/ turn
Itz/ yor/ migh/ turn.

Es /tu/ mi/ turno.

Your piece is in the wrong place.
Yor pees iz in th'rawng pleis.

Tu pieza está mal puesta.

I'll throw the dice now.
Ighl throh th'dighs naou.

Yo tiro los dados ahora.

I want the blue figure. (piece)
Igh wahnt th'bloo FIG-yur.

Yo quiero la figura azul.*

That's not playing fair.
Thatz naht plei'ng fehr.

Eso no es jugar limpio.

You have to pay me.
Yoo hav t'pei mee.

Tienes que pagarme.

Move forward.
Moov FOR-wurd.

Mueve hacia adelante.

Move backward.
Moov BAK-wurd.

Mueve hacia atrás.

You are winning. You won.
Yoo ahr WIN-'ng. Yoo wuhn.

Estás ganando. Ganaste.

You are losing. You lost.
Yoo ahr LOOZ-'ng. Yoo lawst.

Estás perdiendo. Perdiste.

(OBSTACLE GAMES)

JUEGOS de OBSTÁCULOS

Go:
Goh:

Anda:

through the hoop,
throo th'hoop,

por el aro,

around the cabinet, — alrededor del gabinete,
uh-RAOUND th'KAB-in-et,

under the table, — debajo de la mesa,
UHN-der th'TEI-bl,

beside the chair. — al lado de la silla.
bee-SIGHD th'chehr.

Stand behind me, in front of the couch. — Ponte detrás de mí, delante del sofá.
Stand bee-HIGHND mee, in fruhnt uhv'th'kaouch.

(QUIET GAMES) JUEGOS TRANQUILOS

Let's play a quiet game. — Jugamos un juego tranquilo.
Letz plei uh'KWIGH-et geim.

Let's put this piece of the puzzle here. — Vamos a poner este pedazo del rompecabezas aquí. *
Letz put this pees uhv'th'PUHZ-zl heer.

This piece doesn't fit. — Este pedazo no cabe.
This pees DUHZ-nt fit.

Do you think this piece goes here? — ¿Piensas que este pedazo va aquí?
Doo yoo think this pees gohz heer?

What piece is missing? — ¿Qué pedazo falta?
Waht pees iz MIS-'ng?

This puzzle is too/ easy/ difficult/. — Este rompecabezas es demasiado /fácil/ difícil/.
This PUHZ-le iz too/ EE-zee/ DIF-ih-kult/.

Look out the window. — Mira por la ventana.
Luk aout th'WIN-doh.

What do you see? — ¿Qué ves?
Waht doo yoo see?

Guess who!
Ges hoo!

¡Adivina quién es!

I spy with my little eye something that...
(is brown and tall). (a tree)
Igh spigh with migh LIT-le igh SUHM-thing that...
(iz braoun and tawl). (uh'tree)

Espío con mi ojito algo que...
(es marrón y alto). (un árbol)

Do you want to play a game of cards (with me)?
Doo yoo wahnt t'plei uh'geim uhv'kahrdz (with mee)?

¿Quieres jugar una partida de cartas (conmigo)?

You can sort through your collection.
Yoo kan sort throo yor kul-EK-shuhn.

Puedes revisar tu colección.

(DOLLS) MUÑECAS

Feed the doll.
Feed th'dawhl.

Dale de comer a la muñeca. *

Dress the doll.
Dres th'dawl.

Víste a la muñeca.

Lay her down gently.
Lei her daoun JENT-lee.

Acuéstala con cuidado.

Don't drag her on the floor.
Dohnt drag her ahn th'flor.

No la arrastres por el suelo.

Don't spank her so hard.
Dohnt spank her soh hard.

No le pegues a ella tan fuerte.

What is the doll's name?
Waht iz th'dawlz neim?

¿Cómo se llama la muñeca?

You can design a dress on the computer.
Yoo kan dee-ZIGHN uh'dres ahn th'kuhm-PYOO-ter.

Tú puedes diseñar una ropa en la computadora.

(SKATING) **PATINAR**

My skates are dull. They need sharpening.
Migh skeitz ahr duhl. Thei need SHAHRP- 'ng.

Mis patines están desafilados. Necesitan ser afilados. *

Hold on to me. I'll help you skate.
Hohld ahn t'mee. Ighl help yoo skeit.

Agárrate a mí. Te ayudaré a patinar.

Lift your right foot.
Lift yor right fut.

Levanta el pie derecho.

Push with your left foot.
Push with yor left fut.

Empuja con el pie izquierdo.

Skate around the rink.
Skeit uh-ROUND th'rink.

Patina alrededor de la sala de patinar.

You're ready to skate backwards.
Yor RED-ee t'skeit BAK-wurdz.

Estás listo/a/ para patinar hacia atrás.

Skate only in the driveway.
Skeit OHN-lee in th'DRIGHV-wei.

Patina solamente en el camino de entrada.

(PLAYGROUND) **PATIO de RECREO**

Go and hide!
Goh and highd!

¡Anda y escóndete!

Where are you? Where am I?
Wehr ahr yoo? Wehr am igh?

¿Dónde estás? ¿Dónde estoy?

Don't jump off the swing.
Dohnt jump awf th'swing.

No saltes del columpio.

Swing! But don't swing too high.
Swing! Buht dohnt swing too high.

¡Columpiate! Pero no te columpies demasiado fuerte. *

Don't stand on the swing.
Dohnt stand ahn th'swing.
No te levantes en el columpio.

I'll push you gently.
Ighl push yoo JENT-lee.
Te empujaré suavemente.

Don't close your eyes.
Dohnt klohz yor ighz.
No cierres los ojos.

Stand in line.
Stand in lighn.
Haz la cola.

Hold onto the slide.
Hohld AHN-too th'slighd.
Agárrate del tobogán. *

Slide down gently.
Slighd daoun JENT-lee.
Deslízate despacio.

Hold onto the merry-go-round.
Hohld AHN-too th'MEH-ree-goh-raound.
Agárrate del carrusel.

The kite is falling; there's not enough wind.
Th'kight iz FAWL-'ng; thehrz naht ih-NUHF wind.
La cometa está cayéndose; no hay bastante viento.

Hold onto the tail.
Hohld AHN-too th'teil.
Agarra la cola.

Do you want/ to jump rope/ or play with the top/?
Doo yoo wahnt/ t'jump rohp/ or plei with th'tahp/?
¿Quieres/ saltar a la comba/ o jugar co[n] el trompo/?

Shoot the marbles into the circle.
Shoot th'MAHR-blz IN-too th'SIR-kl.
Tira las canicas hacia el círculo.

Blow up the balloon. Air is leaking from it.
Bloh ahp th'bah-LOON. Ehr iz LEEK-'ng fruhm it.
Infla el globo. El aire se está saliendo. *

(COLORING and PASTING) **PINTAR y PEGAR**

Let her use your crayons.
Let her yooz yor KREI-ahnz.
Déjale usar tus crayones. *

Color the sun yellow.
KUHL-er th'suhn YEHL-oh.
Colorea el sol amarillo.

Paint the bird the color you like.
Peint th'burd th'KUHL-er yoo lighk.
Pinta el pájaro del color que te guste.

Draw a picture of daddy.
Draw uh'PIK-chur uhv'DAD-ee.
Haz un dibujo de papi.

Draw the circle, triangle, the square like this.
Draw th'SIR-kl, TRIGH-ang-gl, th'skwehr lighk this.
Dibuja el círculo, el triángulo, el cuadrado así. *

Cut out this picture from the magazine.
Kuht aout this PIK-chur fruhm th'MAG-uh-zeen.
Corta este retrato de la revista.

Paste it carefully on the paper.
Peist it KEHR-fuh-lee ahn th'PEI-per.
Pégalo/ la/ en el papel con cuidado.

Fold the paper/ in two/ in four/.
Fohld th' PEI-per/ in too/ in for/.
Dobla el papel/ en dos partes/ en cuatro partes/.

Don't tear the paper.
Dohnt tehr th'PEI-per.
No rompas el papel.

/Roll/ form/ squeeze/ the clay like this.
/Rohl/ form/ skweez/ th'klei lighk this.
/Rueda/ forma/ aprieta/ la plastelina así.

Clean up your crayons and paper.
Kleen ahp yor KREI-ahnz and PEI-per.
Recoje tus crayones y tu papel.

(TRAINS and TRUCKS) **TRENES y CAMIONES**

All aboard!
Awl uh-BORD!
¡Abordo!

Tickets, please.
TIK-etz, pleez.
Boletos, por favor.

How much is the fare?
Haou muhch iz th'fehr?
¿Cuánto es el pasaje?

When do we arrive in New York?
Wen doo wee uh-RIGHV in nyoo york?
¿Cuándo llegamos a Nueva York?

Are you delivering oil in your oil truck?
Ahr yoo dee-LIV-ring oyl in yor oyl truhk?
¿Repartes aceite en tu camión de aceite?

I'm driving/ backwards/ forwards/.
Ighm DRIGHV-'ng / BAK-wurdz/ FOR-wurdz/.
Yo conduzco/ hacia atrás/ adelante/.

This is not an oil truck; this is a fire engine.
This iz naht an oyl truhk; this iz uh'fighr EN-jin.
Este no es un camión de aceite; es una bomba de incendios.

I want a red pick-up.
Igh wahnt uh'red pik-ahp.
Quiero una camioneta roja.

I'm loading my truck with sand.
Ighm LOHD-'ng migh truhk with sand.
Estoy cargando mi camión con arena. *

I like the five-speed transmission.
Igh lighk th'fighv-speed tranz-MISH-un.
Me gusta la caja de cinco velocidades.

When I get my driver's license...
Wen igh get migh DRIGHV-erz LIGH-sens...
Cuando recibo mi permiso de conducir.

SATURDAY AFTERNOON	SÁBADO *por la* TARDE
Let's go/ see a movie/ to the mall/. *Letz goh/ see uh'MOO-vee/ t'th'mawl/.*	Vámonos / al cine/ al centro comercial/.
Can _______ and ________ come with us? *Kan _______ and ________ kuhm with us?*	¿Pueden venir_____ y______ con nosotros?
I'd rather go to the playground *Ighd RATH-er goh t'th'PLEI-graound.*	Prefiero ir al patio de recreo.
It's more fun. *Itz mor fun.*	Es más divertido.
Meet me/ at the field/ at the country fair/. *Meet mee/ at th'feeld/ at th'KUHN-tree fehr/*	Queda conmigo /al campo/ a la feria/.
Are your chores done? *Ahr yor chorz duhn?*	¿Has terminado las faenas?

Is there anything good on TV?
Iz thehr EN-ee-thing gud ahn tee-vee?

¿Habrá algún buen programa en la tele?

Let's watch the Spanish channel.
Letz wahch th'SPAN-ish CHAN-el.

Mostramos el canal en español.

There's:
Thehrz:

Hay:

a train show,
uh'trein shoh,

un espectáculo de trenes, *

a play at school,
uh'plei at skool,

una obra en la escuela,

a puppet show,
uh'PUP-pet shoh,

un espectáculo de marionetas,

a rock concert.
uh'rahk KAHN-surt.

un concierto de música rock.

We'll take /the subway/ the bus/.
Weel teik /th'SUB-wei/ th'buhs/.

Tomaremos/ el metro/ el autobús/.

I want to try /Mexican food/ fast food/.
Igh wahnt t'trigh/ MEKS-ee-ken food/ fast food/.

Quiero probar /comida mejicana/ comida rápida/.

You have an appointment at the dentist's.
Yoo hav an uh-POYT-ment at th'DENT-ists.

Tienes una cita con el dentista.

Sorry!
SAHR-ee!

¡Lo siento!

Your braces need adjustment.
Yor BREIS-ez need uh-JUHST-ment.

Hay que arreglar los aparatos.

No! You can't get your hair dyed red!
Noh! Yoo kant get yor hehr dighd red!

¡No! ¡No puedes teñirte el pelo rojo!

Hop in, and we'll go for a ride.
Hahp in, and weel goh for uh'righd.

Súbete y vamos a dar un paseo en coche.

Call _________ ,and let's go skateboarding.
Kawl _________, and letz goh SKEIT-bord-'ng.

Llama a _________, y vamos de paseo en monopatín. *

Hang-gliding would be fun!
HANG-glighd-'ng wud bee fun!

¡Vuelo libre sería divertido!

Let's listen to the CD.
Letz LIS-en t'th'see-dee.

Escuchemos el disco compacto.

Would you like to go fishing?
Wud yoo lighk t'goh FISH-'ng?

¿Te gustaría ir a pescar?

I'd rather go fishing.
Ighd RATH-er goh FISH-'ng.

Prefiero ir a pescar. *

We've got the bait, hooks and net.
Weev gaht th'beit, hooks and net.

Tenemos el cebo, los anzuels, y la red.

You forgot the fishing rod.
Yoo for-GAHT th'FISH-'ng rahd.

Te olvidaste de la caña de pescar.

My fishing line is caught on the bottom.
Migh FISH-'ng lighn iz kawt ahn th'BAHT-um.

El hilo de pescar está atascado en el fondo.

I caught two fish!
Igh kawt too fish!

Cogí dos peces!

Can we build the tree house?
Kan wee bild th'tree haous?

¿Podemos construir la casita en el árbol?

Meet me in the back yard.
Meet mee in th'bak yahrd.

Queda conmigo en el jardín.

Let's:
Letz:

Vamos a:

go to the attic,
goh t'th'AT-ik,

ir al desván,

watch/ cartoons/ soccer/ on TV,
wahch/ kahr-TOONZ/ SAHK-er/ ahn tee-vee,

mirar/ dibujos animados/ fútbol/ en la televisión,

read comics,
reed KAHM-iks,

leer las cómicas,

rent a video,
rent uh'VID-ee-oh,

alquilar un vídeo,

go to the/ beach/ lake/,
goh t'th'/ beech/ leik/,

ir/ a la playa/ al lago/,

go to the/ ocean/ pool/,
goh t'th'/ OH-shin/ pool/,

ir/ al océano/ a la piscina/,

go swimming,
goh SWIM-'ng,

nadar,

go waterskiing.
goh WAW-ter-skee-'ng.

esquiar en agua.

I'll bring:
Ighl bring:

Llevo:

my CD's,
migh see-deez,

mis discos compactos,

the towels,
th'taoulz,

las toallas,

the beach umbrella,
th'beech um-BREHL-uh,

la sombrilla,

the beach chair,
th'beech chehr,

la silla de la playa,

the shovel and the pail. *th'SHUV-el and th'peil.*	la pala y el balde. *
Everybody out! *EV-ree-bahd-ee aout!*	¡Todos afuera!
Here we are! *Heer wee ahr!*	¡Aquí estamos!
Let's stay here. There aren't too many people. *Letz stei heer. Thehr AHR-nt too MEN-ee PEE-pl.*	Vamos a quedarnos aquí. No hay demasiada gente.
I prefer the shade. *Igh pree-FER th'sheid.*	Prefiero la sombra.
It's near the/ water/ drink stand/. *Itz neer th'/ WAW-ter/ drink stand/.*	Está cerca del /agua/ puesto de bebidas/.
The water looks clear. *Th'WAW-ter luks kleer.*	El agua parece clara.
Look at the waves! *Luk at th'weivz!*	¡Mira las olas!
The sea is rough! *Th'see iz ruf!*	¡El mar está revuelto!
Why don't you collect some seashells? *Wigh dohnt yoo kuh-LEKT suhm SEE-shelz?*	¿Por qué no recojes algunas conchas de mar? *
You can't go into the water now. You have just eaten lunch *Yoo kant goh IN-too th'WAW-ter naou.* *Yoo hav juhst EET-en luhnch.*	No puedes meterte al agua ahora. Acabas de almorzar.
That speed boat is very close to the buoy. *That speed boht iz VER-ee klohs t'th BOO-ee.*	Ese bote de carrera está muy cerca de la boya. *
Float on your back. *Floht ahn yor bak.*	Flota boca arriba.

Come out of the water.
Kuhm aout uhv'th'WAW-ter.
Sal del agua.

You're shivering with cold.
Yor SHIV-'ring with kohld.
Estás temblando de frío.

Where is the sunblock?
Wehr iz th'suhn-blahk?
¿Dónde está la crema protectora?

I want to get a suntan.
Igh wahnt t'get uh'SUHN-tan.
Quiero ponerme morena.

The sun is/ strong/ hot/.
Th'sun iz/ strawng/ haht/.
El sol está/ fuerte/ caliente/.

There's seaweed on your back.
Thehrz SEE-weed ahn yor bak.
Hay algas en tu espalda.

Build a sand castle.
Bild uh'sand KAS-ul.
Haz un castillo de arena. *

Watch the birds/ come down/ fly/.
Wahch th'burdz/ kuhm daoun/ fligh/.
Mira los pájaros/ bajar/ volar/.

Did you forget your sunglasses?
Did yoo for-GET yor SUHN-glas-ez?
¿Te olvidaste de las gafas de sol? *

When are we leaving?
Wen ahr wee LEEV-'ng?
¿Cuándo salimos?

It's time to go. Let's pack up.
Itz tighm t'goh. *Letz pak ahp.*
Es hora de irnos. Empaquemos.

I had a good time (at the beach).
Igh had uh'gud tighm (at th'beech).
Lo pasé bien (en la playa).

It'a pleasure to go to the beach.
Itz uh PLEH-zhur t'goh t'th'beech.
Es un placer ir a la playa.

Keep an eye on your sister.
Keep an igh ahn yor SIS-ter.
Vigila a tu hermana.

I want to rent...
Igh wahnt t'rent...

Quiero alquilar...

We need to rent ski poles, skis, and boots.
Wee need t'rent skee pohlz, skeez and bootz.

Necesitamos alquilar palos de esquí, esquíes, y botas. *

Are your boots comfortable?
Ahr yor bootz KUHM-fer-tuh-bl?

¿Son cómodas tus botas?

Are your ski poles too/ long/ short/?
Ahr yor skee pohlz too/ lawng/ short/?

¿Son demasiado/ largos/ cortos/ tus palos de esquiar?

Your bindings are too/ loose/ tight/.
Yor BIGHND-'ngz ahr too/ loos/ tight/.

Tus tiras de esquí están demasiado/ sueltas/ apretadas/.

Where do they sell tickets for the ski lift?
Wehr doo thei sel TIK-etz for th'skee lift?

¿Dónde venden boletos para el telesquí?

Don't go to the top of the hill.
Dohnt goh t'th'tahp uhv'th'hil.

No vayas al pico de la montaña.

That hill is a little steep.
That hil iz uh'LIT-le steep.

Esa colina es un poco empinada.

Those skiers go too fast.
Thohz SKEE-erz goh too fast.

Aquellos esquiadores van demasiado rápido.

Look out!
Luk aout!

¡Cuidado!

Don't ski/ too/ so/ fast.
Dohnt skee/ too/ soh/ fast.

No esquíes /demasiado/ tanto/ rápido.

The snow is/ soft/ hard/.
Th'snoh iz /sawft/ hahrd/.

La nieve es/ suave/ dura/.

What form!
Waht form!

¡Qué forma!

You are skiing just fine
Yoo ahr SKEE-'ng juhst fighn.

Estás esquiando muy bien.

Are you tired?
Ahr yoo TIGH-erd?

¿Estás cansado/a/?

Are you/ hungry/ cold/?
Ahr yoo/ HUHN-gree/ kohld/?

¿Tienes/ hambre/ frío/?

I'm/ hungry/ cold/.
Ighm/ HUHN-gree/ kohld/.

Tengo /hambre/ frío/.

Let's go inside to/ rest/ eat/ warm up/.
Letz goh in-SIGHD t'/ rest/ eet/ wahrm ahp/.

Vamos adentro a/ descansar/ comer/ calentarnos/.

Come warm yourself.
Kuhm wahrm yor-SELF.

Ven a calentarte.

It's nice and warm here.
Itz nighs and wahrm heer.

Aquí hace un calorcito muy agradable.

There is going to be a lot of traffic.
Thehr iz GOH-'ng t'bee uh'laht uhv'TRAF-ik.

Va a haber mucho tráfico.

Don't forget anything.
Dohnt for-GET EN-ee-thing.

No olvides cualquier cosa.

Did you forget something?
Did yoo for-GET SUHM-thing?

¿Te olvidaste algo?

Call your parents.
Kawl yor PEHR-entz.

Llama a tus padres.

They are waiting for you to call them.
Thei ahr WEIT-'ng for yoo t'kawl them.

Están esperando que los llames.

Did you have a good time?
Did yoo hav uh'gud tighm?

¿Te divertiste?

¡Le has tocado el gordo! You hit the jackpot!

EXCLAMATIONS !	¡EXCLAMACIONES !
Ah! Wow! Ouch! Whoops! *Ah! Waou! Aouch! Woops!*	¡Ay!
Darn! Wow! *Dahrn! Waou!*	¡Caramba!
It completely slipped my mind! *It kuhm-PLEET-lee slipt migh mighnd!*	¡Se me olvidó por completo!
I am glad. *Ighm glad.*	Me alegro. (or) Estoy alegre.
We are glad that you won. I am sad. *Wee ahr glad that yoo wuhn. Ighm sad.*	Estamos contentos/as de que hayas ganado. Estoy triste.
Help! *Help!*	¡Socorro!
Look out! Go easy! *Luk aout! Goh EE-zee!*	¡Cuidado!

I'm sorry. It's my fault. *Ighm SAHR-ee. Itz migh fawlt.*	Lo siento. Es mi culpa.
It's your fault. *Itz yor fawlt.*	Es culpa tuya.
I didn't understand everything you said. *Igh DID'nt uhn-der-STAND EV-ree-thing yoo sed.*	No entendí todo lo que me dijiste.
Don't remind me! *Dohnt ree-MIGHND mee!*	¡No me hagas acordarme!
I'm sorry that you fell. *Ighm SAHR-ee that yoo fel.*	Siento que te hayas caído.
Well now! *Wel naou!*	¡Pues bien!
Isn't that so? Is that so? *IZ-nt that soh? Iz that soh?*	¿No es verdad? ¿Verdad?
Who cares? *Hoo kehrz?*	¿A quién le importa?
I don't care. *Igh dohnt kehr.*	No me importa.
It doesn't matter. *It DUHZ-'nt MAT-er.*	No importa.
Who knows? *Hoo nohz?*	¿Quién sabe?
Okay. All right. *OH-kei. Awl right.*	Bueno. Está bien.
Of course! *Uhv kors!*	¡Por supuesto!

Of course not! *Uhv'kors naht!*	¡Claro que no!
Certainly! Sure! *SUR-ten-lee! Shuur!*	¡Ciertamente! ¡Seguro!
Without fail! *With-AOUT feil!*	¡Sin duda!
No way! *Noh wei!*	¡De ninguna manera!
How interesting! *Haou IN-ter-est-'ng!*	¡Qué interesante!
How funny! It's funny. *Haou FUN-ee! Itz FUN-ee.*	¡Qué divertido! Es cómico.
What nonsense! *Waht NAHN-sens!*	¡Qué tontería!
Good grief! *Gud greef!*	¡Qué cosa!
I'm not in the mood for jokes. *Ighm naht in th'mood for johks.*	No estoy para bromas.
What luck! You are lucky! *Waht luhk! Yoo ahr LUHK-ee!*	¡Qué suerte! ¡Tienes suerte! *
How awful! *Haou AW-ful!*	¡Qué horrible!
Too bad! What a pity! *Too bad! Waht uh'PIT-ee!*	¡Qué lástima!
How unusual! That's extraordinary! *Haou uhn-YOOZ-'ual! Thatz eks-TRAW-din-ehr-ee!*	¡Qué raro! ¡Es extraordinario!

How kind/ nice! *Haou kighnd/ nighs!*	¡Qué simpatico/ a/!
Marvelous! Wonderful! *MAHR-vel-us! WUHN-dr-ful!*	¡Maravilloso!
You saved my life! *Yoo savd migh lighf!*	¡Me salvastes la vida!
You're the greatest! *Yor th'GREIT-est!*	¡Eres el mejor!
What a joke! *Waht uh'johk!*	¡Qué chiste!
I should say so! *Igh shud sei soh!*	¡Claro que sí!
It's out of the question! *Itz aout uhv'th'KWES-tyuhn !*	¡Es imposible!
It's impossible! It can't be! *Itz im-PAH-sih-bl! It kant bee!*	¡No puede ser!
Don't worry. *Dohnt WUR-ee.*	No te preocupes.
It could happen to anyone. *It kud HAP-en t'EN-ee-wuhn.*	Le podría pasar a cualquiera.
It's all right. That's fine. *Itz awl right. Thatz fighn.*	Está bien.
It's not right. It's not fair. *Itz naht right. Itz naht fehr.*	No es correcto. No es justo.
I smell a rat! *Igh smel uh'rat!*	¡Aquí hay gato encerrado!
That's it! *Thatz it!*	¡Eso es!

That is not necessary. *That iz naht NES-uh-sehr-ee.*	No es necesario.
All gone! *Awl gahn!*	¡Todo terminado!
Up you go! *Ahp yoo goh!*	¡Upah!
Look at the mess! *Luk at th'mes!*	¡Mira qué desorden!
That's true! Is that so? *Thatz troo! Iz that soh?*	¡Es verdad! ¿Es verdad?
I hope/ so/ not/! *Igh hohp/ soh/ naht/!*	¡Espero que /sí/ no/!
I think/ so/ not/! *Igh think/ soh/ naht/!*	¡Creo que /sí/ no/!
Well...Then... Let me see... *Wel...Then... Let mee see...*	Pues… Entonces... A ver...
Well now! *Wel naou!*	¡Ahora bien!
Indeed! You don't say! *In-DEED! Yoo dohnt sei!*	¡De veras! ¡No me digas!
What? *Waht?*	¿Qué?
As usual… *As YOOZ-u'al...*	Como siempre...
What a sneeze! God bless you! *Waht uh'sneez! Gahd bles yoo!*	¡Qué estornudo! ¡Salud!
How you frown! *Haou yoo fraoun!*	¡Qué mala cara pones!

¡EXCLAMACIONES !

What is wrong? *Waht iz rawng?*	¿Qué pasa?
What is the matter with you? *Waht iz th'MAT-er with yoo?*	¿Qué te pasa?
Why are you/ complaining/ angry/? *Wigh ahr yoo/ kuhm-PLEIN-'ng/ AN-gree/?*	¿Por qué/ te quejas/ estás enojado/ a?
For goodness sake! *For GUD-nes seik!*	¡Por Dios!
This is no laughing matter! *This iz noh LAFF-'ng MAT-er!*	¡Esto no es para reírte!
It serves you right! *It servz yoo right!*	¡Lo mereces!
You must not say that! *Yoo muhst naht sei that!*	¡No debes decir eso!
God forbid! *Gahd for-BID!*	¡Dios me ampare!
Why on earth! *Wigh ahn erth!*	¡Por el amor de Dios!
It's immense! *Itz ee-MENS!*	¡Es inmenso/ a/!
That's fine! *Thatz fighn!*	¡Está bien!
Stop it! *Stahp it!*	¡ Déjalo!
Go and be happy. *Goh and bee HAP-ee.*	Ve y sé feliz.

BIRTHDAY PARTY	FIESTA *de* CUMPLEAÑOS

What would you like for your birthday?
Waht *wud yoo lighk for yor BIRTH-dei?*

¿Qué te gustaría para tu cumpleaños?

Would you like to have a party:
Wud yoo lighk t'hav uh'PAHR-tee:

¿Te gustaría tener una fiesta:

at home,
at hohm,

en casa,

at a restaurant,
at uh'REST-rahnt,

en un restaurante,

at the park,
at th'pahrk,

en el parque,

or at the beach?
or at th'beech?

o a la playa?

We'll invite your friends.
Weel in-VIGHT yor frendz.

Invitaremos a tus amigos/as/.

We will have cake, ice cream, hats, games and presents.
Wee wil hav keik, ighs kreem, hatz, geimz and PREH-zentz.

Tendremos un pastel, helado, sombreritos, juegos y regalos. *

How old are you?
Haou ohld ahr yoo?

¿Cuántos años tienes?

I am five years old.
Igh am fighv yirz ohld.

Tengo cinco años.

I don't know.
Igh dohnt noh.

No sé.

I was born...(October 5th).
Igh wuhz bawrn...(ahk-TOH-br fifth).

Yo nací ...(el 5 de octubre)

Blow out the candles of the cake.
Bloh aout th'KAN-dlz uhv'th'keik.

Sopla las velitas del pastel. *

What a pretty birthday card!
Waht uh'PRI-tee BIRTH-dei kahrd!

¡Qué bonita tarjeta de cumpleaños!

Cut the birthday cake.
Kuht th'BIRTH-dei keik.

Corta la tarta de cumpleaños.

Divide the cake into eight pieces.
Dih-VIGHD th'keik IN-too eit PEE-sez.

Divide el pastel en ocho pedazos.

What a nice party!
Waht uh'nighs PAHR-tee!

¡Qué buena fiesta!

BEDTIME	HORA de ACOSTARSE

What a yawn!
Waht uh'yawn!

¡Qué bostezo!

You are/ yawning/ tired/?
Yoo ahr/ YAWN-'ng/ TIGHR-ed/?

¿Estás/ bostezando/ cansado/?

It's time for bed.
Itz tighm for bed.

Es hora de irse a la cama.

Are you sleepy?
Ahr yoo SLEEP-ee?

¿Tienes sueño?

I am putting you to bed
Igh am PUT-'ng yoo t'bed.

Te estoy acostando.

Do you want me to put you to bed?
Doo yoo wahnt mee t'put yoo t'bed?

¿Quieres que yo te acueste?

Go get your book. *Goh get yor buk.*	Busca tu libro.
I'll read you a story before you go to bed. *Ighl reed yoo uh'STOR-ee bee-FOR yoo goh t'bed.*	Te leeré un cuento antes de que te acuestes.
I'll go get my book. *Ighl goh get migh buk.*	Voy por mi libro.
Do you have permission to watch television? *Doo yoo hav per-MISH-uhn t'wahch TEL-uh -VIZH-uhn?*	¿Tienes permiso para mirar la televisión?
I find this program a little boring. *Igh fighnd this PROH-gram uh'LIT-le BOR-'ng.*	Encuentro este programa un tanto aburrido.
Take off your clothes. *Teik awf yor klohz.*	Quítate la ropa.
Put on your pajamas. *Put ahn yor pah-JAHM-ahz.*	Ponte el pijama. *
Hang your shirt on the hanger. *Hang yor shirt ahn th'HANG-er.*	Cuelga la camisa en la percha.
Put all your clothes away. *Put awl yor klohz uh-WEI.*	Guarda toda la ropa.
These socks need laundering. *Theez sahks need LAWND-ring.*	Estos calcetines necesitan ser lavados. *
Are you ready for bed? *Ahr yoo RED-ee for bed?*	¿Estás listo/ a/ para la cama?
Say "Goodnight" to daddy. *Sei "Gud-NIGHT" t'DAD-ee.*	Dile, "buenas noches" a papi.
Did you say your prayers? *Did yoo sei yor prehrz?*	¿Dijiste las oraciones?

You are heavy.
Yoo ahr HEV-ee.

Estás pesado.

Close your eyes. Go to sleep.
Klohz yor ighz. Goh t'sleep.

Cierra los ojos. Duérmete.

Be still. Be quiet.
Bee stil. Bee KWIGH-et.

Estate tranquilo. Estate quieto.

Sleep well.
Sleep wel.

Que duermas bien.

You have to sleep now.
Yoo hav t'sleep naou.

Tienes que dormir ahora.

Pleasant dreams.
PLEZ-ent dreemz.

Que duermas con los angelitos.

You must stay in bed.
Yoo muhst stei in bed.

Tienes que quedarte en la cama.

You are not in bed yet?
Yoo ahr naht in bed yet?

¿No estás en la cama todavía?

It is not too early to go to bed.
It iz naht too EHR-lee t'goh t'bed.

No es demasiado temprano para acostarte.

Do you want the light lit?
Doo yoo wahnt th'light lit?

¿Quieres la luz encendida?

Mommy loves you.
MAH-mee luhvz yoo.

Mami te quiere.

Give me a kiss.
Giv mee uh'kis.

Dame un beso.

God bless you.
Gahd bles yoo.

Dios te bendiga.

HORA *de* ACOSTARSE

Are you wet?
Ahr yoo wet?

¿Estás mojado/a/?

Are you/ awake/ asleep/?
Ahr yoo/ uh-WEIK/ uh-SLEEP/?

¿Estás/ despierto/ a/ dormido/ a/?

/She/ He/ is sleeping.
/Shee/ Hee/ iz SLEEP-'ng.

/Ella/ Él/ está durmiendo.

Why are you not yet asleep?
Wigh ahr yoo naht yet uh-SLEEP?

¿Por qué no estás dormido/ a todavía?

Can't you fall asleep?
Kant yoo fawl uh-SLEEP?

¿No puedes dormirte?

Don't wake/ him/ her/.
Dohnt weik/ him/her/.

No/ lo/ la/ despiertes.

What do you want, my little one?
Waht doo yoo wahnt, migh LIT-le wuhn?

¿Qué quieres, mi hijito/ a/?

You scratched your face in your sleep.
Yoo skracht yor feis in yor sleep.

Te raspaste la cara cuando estabas dormido.

Are you bleeding? I'm bleeding.
Ahr yoo BLEED-'ng? Ighm BLEED-'ng.

¿Te estás sangrando? Me desangro.

Don't you feel well?
Dohnt yoo feel wel?

¿No te sientes bien?

Are you/ dizzy/ sick/?
Ahr yoo/ DIZ-ee/ sik/?

¿Estás / mareado/ a/ enfermo/ a/?

You have/ a fever/ the flu/.
Yoo hav/ uh'FEEV-er/ th'floo/.

Tienes / fiebre/ la gripe/.

You have spots on your chest. (Chicken pox).
Yoo hav spahtz ahn yor chehst. (CHIK-en pahks).

Tienes manchitas en el pecho. (Varicela)

Your glands are swollen.
Yor glandz ahr SWOH-len.

Tus glándulas están hinchadas.

Stick out your tongue.
Stik aout yor tung.

Saca la lengua.

You have a cold. You're coughing.
Yoo hav uh'kohld. Yor KAWF-'ng.

Tienes un resfriado. Estás tosiendo.

You'll need something for that cough.
Yool need SUHM-thing for that kawf.

Necesitas algo para la tos.

Cover your mouth when you cough.
KUHV-er yor maouth wen yoo kawf.

Tapate la boca cuando toses.

Tomorrow you'll have to stay in bed.
Tub-MAHR-oh yool hav t'stei in bed.

Mañana tendrás que quedarte en la cama.

Does your/ arm/ foot/ hurt?
Duhz yor/ ahrm/ fut/ hurt?

¿Te duele/ el brazo/el pie/?

Do you want a bandaid (for your finger)?
Doo yoo wahnt uh'BAND-eid (for yor FING-er)?

¿Quieres una curita (para el dedo)?

*

WEATHER	El TIEMPO

It's light.
Itz light.

Ya está claro.

It's sunny.
Itz SUHN-ee

Hace sol. *

There are no clouds.
Thehr ahr noh klaoudz.

No hay nubes.

The sun is shining.
Th'suhn iz SHIGHN-'ng.

Brilla el sol.

It's/ hot/ warm / today.
Itz/ haht/ wahrm/ tuh-DEI.

Hace/ mucho calor/ calor/ hoy.

It's terribly hot. It's summer.
Itz TEHR-uh-blee haht. Itz SUHM-er.

Hace un calor terrible. Es verano.

We're having a heat wave.
Weer HAV-'ng uh'heet weiv.

Tenemos una ola de calor.

There's not (even) a breath of wind.
Thehrz naht (EE-ven) uh'breth uhv'wind.

No hay ni un respiro de viento.

It's (very) windy.
Itz (VER-ee) WIND-ee.

Hace (mucho) viento.

What a beautiful night.
Waht uh'BYOO-ti-ful night.

Qué linda noche.

It's/ cool/ cold/.
Itz/ kool/ kohld/.

Hace/ fresco/ frío/.

You need a/ coat/ sweater/.
Yoo need uh/ koht/ SWEHT-er/.

Necesitas un/ abrigo/ súeter/.

It's (sort of) cloudy.
Itz (sort uhv) KLAOU-dee.

Está (medio) nublado.

It's raining.
Itz REIN-'ng.

Llueve. (o) Está lloviendo.

It's pouring (cats and dogs).
Itz POR-'ng (katz and dawgz).

Está cayendo un chaparrón.

Raindrops are falling.
REIN-drahps ahr FAWL-'ng.

Gotas de lluvia están cayendo.

Look at the rain.
Luk at th'rein.

Mira la lluvia.

The street is full of puddles.
Th'street iz ful uhv' PUD-lz.

La calle está llena de charcos. *

Take off your shoes.
Teik awf yor shooz.

Quítate los zapatos.

Your feet are wet.
Yor feet ahr wet.

Tus pies están mojados.

What an unpleasant day
Waht an un-PLEZ-ent dei.

Qué día tan féo.

What awful weather.
Waht AW-ful WETH-er.

Qué mal tiempo.

What nasty weather!
Waht NAS-tee WETH-er!

¡Qué tiempo tan horrible!

The weather is bad.
Th'WETH-er iz bad.

El tiempo está malo.

It will be dark soon.
It wil bee dahrk soon.

Pronto va a estar oscuro.

It's getting dark.
Itz GET- 'ng dahrk.

Está oscureciendo.

The sky is/ dark/ gray/.
Th'skigh iz/ dahrk/ grei/.

El cielo está /oscuro/ gris/.

There's thunder and lightning.
Thehrz THUHN-dr and LIGHT-n'ng.

Hay truenos y relámpagos. *

What a storm!
Waht uh'storm!

¡Qué tormenta!

What fog!
Waht fahg!

¡Qué niebla! (o) ¡Qué neblina!

Wait until the rain stops.
Weit un-TIL th'rein stahps.

Espera hasta que pare la lluvia.

Look (at the rainbow)!
Luk (at th'REIN-boh)!

¡Mira (el arcoiris)!

It's a real winter day
Itz uh'reel WIN-ter dei.

Es un verdadero día de invierno.

It's beginning to snow.
Itz bee-GIN-'ng t'snoh.

Está empezando a nevar.

It's snowing.
Itz SNOH-'ng.

Está nevando. (o) Nieva.

Snowflakes are falling.
SNOH-fleiks ahr FAWL-'ng.

Están cayendo copitos de nieve.

Look at the snow.
Luk at th'snoh.

Mira la nieve.

How the snow sparkles!
Haou th'snoh SPAHRK-klz!

¡Cómo brilla la nieve!

Perhaps we can make a snowman.
Per-HAPS wee kan meik uh'SNOH-man.

Quizás podemos hacer un muñeco de nieve.

The/ snow/ rain/ has stopped.
Th'/snoh/ rein/ haz stahpt.

Ha dejado/ de nevar/ de llover/.

The snow is melting.
Th'snoh iz MELT-'ng.

La nieve se está descongelando.

What a beautiful day!
Waht uh'BYOO-ti-ful dei!

¡Qué lindo día!

Más vale tarde que nunca. Better late than never.

TIME	*La* HORA
It's one o'clock. *Itz wuhn oh-KLAHK.*	Es la una.
It's two o'clock. *Itz too oh-KLAHK.*	Son las dos.
It's three fifteen. *Itz three FIF-teen.*	Son las tres y cuarto.
It's four thirty. *Itz for THIR-tee.*	Son las cuatro y media.
It's four forty-five. *Itz for FOR-tee-fighv.*	Son las cinco menos cuarto.
It's six twenty. *Itz siks TWEN-tee.*	Son las seis y veinte.

It's six forty. *Itz siks FOR-tee.*	Son las siete menos veinte.
It's eight o'clock. *Itz eit oh-KLAHK.*	Son las ocho.
It's nine o'clock. *Itz nighn oh-KLAHK.*	Son las nueve.
It's ten o'clock. *Itz ten oh-KLAHK.*	Son las diez.
It's eleven o'clock. *Itz ee-LEV-en oh-KLAHK.*	Son las once.
It's midnight. *Itz MID-night.*	Es medianoche.
It's noon. *Itz noon.*	Es mediodía.
It's morning. *Itz MORN-'ng.*	Es de mañana.
It's afternoon. *Itz AF-ter-noon.*	Es de tarde.
It's night(time), evening. *Itz night, EEV-ning.*	Es de noche.
It's/ early/ late/. *Itz/ EHR-lee/ leit/.*	Es/ temprano/ tarde/.
It's getting late. *Itz GET-'ng leit.*	Se hace tarde.
A short while. *Uh'short wighl.*	Un rato.
As soon as possible. *Az soon az PAHS-ih-bl.*	Lo antes posible.

QUANTITIES	CANTIDADES

How old are you?
Haou ohld ahr yoo?

¿Cuántos años tienes?

How old is/ mommy/daddy/?
Haou ohld iz/ MAHM-ee/ DAD-ee/?

¿Cuántos años tiene/ mami/ papi/?

How many fingers do you see?
Haou MEN-ee FING-erz doo yoo see?

¿Cuántos dedos ves?

How many are there?
Haou MEN-ee ahr thehr?

¿Cuántos hay?

There is only one of them.
Thehr iz OHN-lee wuhn uhv'them.

Hay solamente uno de ellos.

There are only four of them.
Thehr ahr OHN-lee for uhv'them.

Hay solamente cuatro de ellos.

I have none (of them).
Igh hav nun (uhv'them).

No tengo ninguno (de ellos).

There are none.
Thehr ahr nuhn.

No hay ninguno.

Put each one in its place.
Put eech wuhn in itz pleis.

Pon cada uno en su lugar.

All the cookies have been eaten.
Awl th'KUK-eez hav ben EET-en.

Todas las galletitas han sido comidas.

There are no more cookies.
Thehr ahr noh mor KUK-eez.

No hay más galletitas.

After fifteen comes sixteen.
AF-ter FIF-teen kuhmz SIKS-teen.

Después de quince viene dieciseis.

One and one make two.
Wuhn and wuhn meik too.

Uno más uno son dos.

Count from three to ten.
Kauunt fruhm three t'ten.

Cuenta de tres a diez.

Four minus three make one.
For MIGHN-uhs three meik wuhn.

Cuatro menos tres son uno.

Two times one make two.
Too tighmz wuhn meik too.

Dos por uno son dos.

Six divided by two make three.
Siks dee-VIGHD-ed bigh too meik three.

Seis dividido por dos son tres.

Two, four, six are even numbers.
Too, for, siks ahr EEV-en NUHM-berz.

Dos, cuatro, seis son números pares.

Three, five, seven are odd numbers.
Three, fighv, SEV-en ahr ahd NUHM-berz.

Tres, cinco, siete son números impares.

two halves
too havz

dos mitades

one half, one third, one fourth *wuhn haf, wuhn third, wuhn forth*	una mitad, un tercio, un cuarto
a little/ more/ less/ *uh'LIT-le/ mor/ lehs/*	un poco/ más/ menos/
some *suhm*	algunos/as (o) unos/as
a few *uh'fyoo*	unos/as (o) pocos/as
many, a lot, several *MEN-ee, uh'laht, SEV-rahl*	muchos/as
enough *ih-NUHF*	bastante

zero *ZEER-oh*	0	seven *SEV-en*	7
one *wuhn*	1	eight *eit*	8
two *too*	2	nine *nighn*	9
three *three*	3	ten *ten*	10
four *for*	4	eleven *ee-LEV-en*	11
five *fighv*	5	twelve *twelv*	12
six *siks*	6	thirteen *THIR-teen*	13

fourteen *FOR-teen*	14	forty *FOR-tee*	40
fifteen *FIF-teen*	15	forty-one *FOR-tee-wuhn*	41
sixteen *SIKS-teen*	16	fifty *FIF-tee*	50
seventeen *SEV-en-teen*	17	fifty-one *FIF-tee-wuhn*	51
eighteen *EI-teen*	18	fifty-two *FIF-tee-too*	52
nineteen *NIGHN-teen*	19	fifty-three *FIF-tee-three*	53
twenty *TWEN-tee*	20	sixty *SIKS-tee*	60
twenty-one *TWEN-tee-wuhn*	21	seventy *SEV-en-tee*	70
twenty-two *TWEN-tee-too*	22	seventy-one *SEV-en-tee-wuhn*	71
twenty-three *TWEN-tee-three*	23	eighty *EI-tee*	80
thirty *THIR-tee*	30	eighty-one *EI-tee-wuhn*	81
thirty-one *THIR-tee-wuhn*	31	ninety *NIGHN-tee*	90
thirty-two *THIR-tee-too*	32	ninety-one *NIGHN-tee-wuhn*	91
thirty-three *THIR-tee-three*	33	ninety-two *NIGHN-tee-too*	92

CANTIDADES

one hundred 100
wuhn HUHN-dred

one hundred one 101
wuhn HUHN-dred wuhn

one hundred two 102
wuhn HUHN-dred too

two hundred 200
too HUHN-dred

two hundred one 201
too HUHN-dred wuhn

three hundred 300
three HUHN-dred

four hundred 400
for HUHN-dred

five hundred 500
fighv HUHN-dred

six hundred 600
siks HUHN-dred

seven hundred 700
SEV-en HUHN-dred

eight hundred 800
eit-HUHN-dred

nine hundred 900
nighn HUHN-dred

one thousand 1000
wuhn THAOU-zen

one thousand five hundred 1500
wuhn THAOU-zen fighv HUHN-dred

two thousand 2000
too THAOU-zen

three thousand five hundred five 3,505
three THAOU-zen fighv HUHN-dred fighv

one hundred thousand 100,000
wuhn HUHN-dred THAOU-zen

one million 1,000,000
wuhn MIL-yuhn

2 million 2,000,000
too MIL-yuhn

Se aprenda con la práctica. Practice makes perfect.

ALPHABET	ALFABETO

A	B	C	D	E	F	G
ei	bee	see	dee	ee	ef	jee
H	I	J	K	L	M	N
eich	igh	jei	kei	el	em	en
O	P	Q	R	S	T	U
oh	pee	kyoo	ahr	es	tee	yoo
V	W		X	Y	Z	
vee	DUH-bl-yoo		eks	wigh	zee	

What letter is this?
Waht LET-er iz this?

¿Qué letra es esta?

Here is the letter A.
Heer iz th'LET-er "ei."

Aquí está la letra A.

Read this letter. *Reed this LET-er.*	Lee esta letra.
How many letters are there in the word cat? *Haou MEN-ee LET-erz ahr thehr in th'wurd kat?*	¿Cuántas letras hay en la palabra gato?
Where is the letter H? *Wehr iz th'LET-er "eich"?*	¿Dónde está la letra H?
Point to the letter J. *Poynt t'th'LET-er "jei."*	Indica la letra J.
What does this word mean? *Waht duhz this wurd meen?*	¿Qué significa esta palabra?
Whose name is this? *Hooz neim iz this?*	¿De quién es este nombre?
Don't hold your pencil so tightly. *Dohnt hohld yor PEN-sil soh TIGHT-lee.*	No agarres el lápiz tan fuerte.
Hold it like this. *Hohld it lighk this.*	Agárralo así.
Write down and then to the right for L. *Right daoun and then t'th'right for "el."*	Escribe hacia abajo y después hacia la derecha para la L.

NURSERY RHYMES — CANCIONES INFANTILES

Nursery rhymes are a marvelous way to learn English or any language. Hearing these rhymes will also give the listener a feel for the rhythm of the language. The feeling of the rhymes are, for the most part, the same whether in Spanish or English.

TO MARKET, TO MARKET

TO MARKET, TO MARKET,
TO BUY A FAT PIG,
HOME AGAIN, HOME AGAIN,
JIGGETY JIG.

TO MARKET, TO MARKET,
TO BUY A FAT HOG,
HOME AGAIN, HOME AGAIN,
JIGGETY JOG!

A la feria, a la feria

Vamos a la feria
un cerdito a comprar.
Ahora lo llevamos
a casa a cuidar.

Vamos a la feria
un gran puerco a vender.
¡Otra vez a casa
para bien comer!

RAIN, RAIN

RAIN, RAIN, GO AWAY,
COME AGAIN ANOTHER DAY;
LITTLE JOHNNY WANTS TO PLAY.

Lluvia, lluvia

Lluvia, lluvia,
vete de aquí.
Vete a Escocia.
No me mojes a mí.

THE THREE LITTLE KITTENS

THE THREE LITTLE KITTENS
THEY LOST THEIR MITTENS,
AND THEY BEGAN TO CRY,
OH, MOTHER DEAR, WE SADLY FEAR
THAT WE HAVE LOST OUR MITTENS.

WHAT! LOST YOUR MITTENS,
YOU NAUGHTY KITTENS!
THEN YOU SHALL HAVE NO PIE!
MEOW, MEOW, MEOW, MEOW.
NO, YOU SHALL HAVE NO PIE!

THE THREE LITTLE KITTENS
THEY FOUND THEIR MITTENS,
AND THEY BEGAN TO CRY,
OH, MOTHER DEAR, SEE HERE, SEE HERE,
THAT WE HAVE FOUND OUR MITTENS.

PUT ON YOUR MITTENS,
YOU SILLY KITTENS,
AND YOU SHALL HAVE SOME PIE.
PURR, PURR, PURR, PURR,
OH, LET US HAVE SOME PIE!

Los tres gatitos

Los tres gatitos
perdieron sus guantecitos
y se pusieron a llorar.
Mamá, mamá, tenemos que confesar
que los guantes se han perdido.

¡Qué malos gatitos,
perder los guantecitos!
Por eso, no tendréis pastel.
Miau, miau, miau, miau.
¡Pues no, no tendréis pastel!

Los tres gatitos
encontraron sus guantecitos
y de nuevo se pusieron a llorar.
Mamá, mamá, ya te podemos avisar
que los acabamos de encontrar.

Poneos los guantecitos,
majaderos gatitos,
y os daré un pastel.
Ronrón, ronrón, ronrón, ronrón.
¡Qué rico es nuestro pastel!

HUMPTY DUMPTY

HUMPTY DUMPTY SAT ON A WALL;
HUMPTY DUMPTY HAD A GREAT FALL;
ALL THE KING'S HORSES,
AND ALL THE KING'S MEN
COULDN'T PUT HUMPTY TOGETHER AGAIN.

Jamti Damti

Jamti Damti se sentó en un muro.
Jamti Damti se cayó muy duro.
Ni la Guardia Civil ni la Caballería
supieron como se incorporaría.

THREE BLIND MICE

THREE BLIND MICE!
THREE BLIND MICE!
SEE HOW THEY RUN! SEE HOW THEY RUN!
THEY ALL RAN AFTER THE FARMER' S WIFE,
WHO CUT OFF THEIR TAILS
WITH A CARVING KNIFE.
DID YOU EVER SEE SUCH A SIGHT
IN YOUR LIFE
AS THREE BLIND MICE?
THREE BLIND MICE?

Los tres ratones ciegos

¡Mira cómo corren,
los tres ratones ciegos!
Que corren y que corren
tras la mujer del granjero
que les corta el rabo
con cuchillo de carnicero.
¿Has visto en tu vida
tales majaderos?
¡Los tres ratones ciegos, los tres
ratones ciegos!

LITTLE MISS MUFFET

LITTLE MISS MUFFET
SAT ON HER TUFFET,
EATING HER CURDS AND WHEY;

ALONG CAME A SPIDER
AND SAT DOWN BESIDE HER,
AND FRIGHTENED MISS MUFFET AWAY.

La señorita Manguito

La señorita Manguito
se sentó en su moñito
a saborear su horchata de chufa.

Un gran alacrán
bajó de un desván
y amargó a la Manguito su afán.

TOMMY TITTLEMOUSE

LITTLE TOMMY TITTLEMOUSE
LIVED IN A LITTLE HOUSE;
HE CAUGHT FISHES
IN OTHER MEN'S DITCHES.

Tomasito Tinto

Tomasito Tinto, pescador de España,
vivía en su chiquita cabaña,
atrapando peces como un ladrón
de las aguas de su patrón.

LITTLE BO-PEEP

LITTLE BO-PEEP HAS LOST HER SHEEP,
AND CAN'T TELL WHERE TO FIND THEM;
LEAVE THEM ALONE,
AND THEY' LL COME HOME,
WAGGING THEIR TAILS BEHIND THEM.

LITTLE BO-PEEP FELL FAST ASLEEP,
AND DREAMT SHE HEARD THEM BLEATING;
BUT WHEN SHE AWOKE,
SHE FOUND IT A JOKE,
FOR STILL THEY ALL WERE FLEETING.

THEN UP SHE TOOK HER LITTLE CROOK,
DETERMINED FOR TO FIND THEM;
SHE FOUND THEM INDEED,
BUT IT MADE HER HEART BLEED,
FOR THEY'D LEFT ALL THEIR TAILS
BEHIND'EM!

IT HAPPENED ONE DAY,
AS BO-PEEP DID STRAY
UNTO A MEADOW HARD BY --
THERE SHE ESPIED THEIR TAILS SIDE BY SIDE,
ALL HUNG ON A TREE TO DRY.

SHE HEAVED A SIGH AND WIPED HER EYE,
AND OVER THE HILLOCKS SHE RACED;
AND TRIED WHAT SHE COULD,
AS A SHEPHERDESS SHOULD,
THAT EACH TAIL SHOULD BE PROPERLY
PLACED.

La pequeño Bo Pip

A la pequeño Bo Pip
se le fue el rebaño
y ya no enquentra la pista.
Dejadlos tranquilos, y vendrán
solitos,
llevando la cola a la vista.

Bo Pip, antes de salir, se puso a
dormir
y soñó que los oía balando;
pero cuando se despertó,
vió que era un engaño
y que sus ovejas andaban vagando.

Cogió en firme su cayado
para salir a buscarlas;
pero cuando las encontró,
se desmayó
porque habían perdido la cola.

Sucedió que un día,
cuando Bo Pip andaba
en un prado de ese lugar,
encontró las colas en fila,
tendidas a sacar.

Suspiró con alivio,
se secó una lagrimita
y salió por el monte dando salitos,
sabiendo que era su debercito
juntar cada cola con su corderito.

Padre Nuestro

Padre nuestro, que estás en el cielo,
santificado sea tu nombre;
venga tu reino,
hágase tu voluntad
en la tierra como en el cielo.
Danos hoy nuestro pan de cada día;
perdona nuestras ofensas como también
nosotros perdonamos a los que nos ofenden;
no nos dejes caer en la tentación,
y líbranos del mal. Amén

Our Father

Our Father who art in heaven,
hallowed be thy name;
thy kingdom come,
thy will be done
on earth as it is in heaven.
Give us this day our daily bread;
forgive us our trespasses as we
forgive those who trespass against us;
and lead us not into temptation,
but deliver us from evil. Amen.

Salmo 23

El Señor es mi pastor;
nada me faltará.
En prados de tiernos pastos
me hace descansar.
Junto a aguas tranquilas me conduce.
Confortará mi alma
y me guiará por sendas de justicia
por amor de su nombre.

Aunque ande en valle de sombra de muerte,
no temeré mal alguno,
porque tú estarás conmigo.
Tu vara y tu cayado me infundirán aliento.

Preparas mesa delante de mí
en presencia de mis adversarios.
Unges mi cabeza con aceite;
mi copa está rebosando.

Ciertamente el bien y la misericordia
me seguirán todos los días de mi vida,
y en la casa del Señor
moraré por días sin fin.

Psalm 23

The Lord is my shepherd;
there is nothing I shall want.
In verdant pastures
He gives me repose.
Beside restful waters He leads me;
He refreshes my soul.
He guides me in right paths
for his name's sake.

Though I walk in the dark valley
I will fear no evil;
for you are at my side.
Your rod and staff give me courage.

You prepare the table before me
in the sight of my foes;
You anoint my head with oil;
my cup overflows.

Only goodness and kindness will
follow me all the days of my life;
And I shall dwell in the house
of the Lord forever.

Oración antes de Comer

Bendícenos, Señor, a nosotros y estos
dones tuyos que vamos a tomar y que
hemos recibido de tu generosidad. Amén.

Prayer before Meals

Bless us, O Lord, and these
your gifts which we are about to
receive from your bounty. Amen.

VOCABULARY

The Family and Other Persons

mami, mamá/ madre	mommy/mother
papi, papá/ padre	daddy/father
la abuela	grandmother
el abuelo	grandfather
la abuelita	grandma
el abuelito	grandpa
la tía	aunt
el tío	uncle
la prima	cousin (f)
el primo	cousin (m)
la sobrina	niece
el sobrino	nephew
la nieta	granddaughter
el nieto	grandson
la hija	daughter
el hijo	son
la hermana	sister
el hermano	brother
la mujer, la señora	woman
el hombre, el señor	man
la chica, la muchacha	girl
el chico, el muchacho	boy
los chicos, los muchachos	children
Señor	Mister
Señora	Missus
Señorita	Miss

Endearments

mi bebé	my baby
mi muñeca	my doll
mi princesa	my princess
mi principito	my little prince
mi tesoro	my treasure
cariño (a)	sweetheart
mi querido (a)	my dear
mi chiquito (a)	my little one
mi vida	my life
mi cielo	my sky
mi corazón	my heart

Colors

amarillo	yellow
avano	beige
azul	blue
blanco	white
café	brown (med)
gris	gray
marrón	brown (dark)
morado	purple
naranja	orange
negro	black
rojo	red
rosa	pink
violeta	violet
verde	green

Days of the Week

el lunes	Monday
el martes	Tuesday
el miércoles	Wednesday
el jueves	Thursday
el viernes	Friday
el sábado	Saturday
el domingo	Sunday

Months of the Year

enero	January
febrero	February
marzo	March
abril	April
mayo	May
junio	June
julio	July
agosto	August

septiembre	September
octubre	October
noviembre	November
diciembre	December

Seasons of the Year

el invierno	winter
la primavera	spring
el verano	summer
el otoño	autumn

Holidays of the Year

el cumpleaños	birthday
el cumpleaños de Jorge Washington	George Washington-ton's Birthday
el cumpleaños de Abraham Lincoln	Abraham Lincoln's Birthday
el día de San Valentín	St. Valentine's Day
el día de San Patricio	St. Patrick's Day
Pascua (de los judios)	Passover
Pascua	Easter (season)
Semana Santa	Easter (Holy)Week
Domingo de Resurreción	Easter Sunday
el día de las madres	Mother's Day
el día de los padres	Father's Day
el cuatro de julio	July 4th
el doce de octubre	October 12th
la víspera de Todos los Santos	Halloween
el día de acción de gracias	Thanksgiving Day
la Navidad	Christmas
la víspera de Año Nuevo	New Year's Eve

Nursery

la bañera	bathtub
la cama con barandas	crib
el chupete	pacifier
el coche del bebé	carriage
el cochecito	stroller
el corral	play pen
el cuadro	picture
la cuna	crib
el juguete	toy
el libro	book
la lámpara de noche	night light
Madre Oca	Mother Goose
la mamadera	feeding bottle
la mecedora	rocker
el pañal	diaper
el pañal desechable	Pamper
la silla alta	high chair

Toys

la alcancía	piggy bank
el anillo	ring
el arete	earring
el aro	hoop
el autobús	bus
el avión (a chorro)	plane (jet)
el bate	bat
la bicicleta	bicycle
la bolita	bead
el bote (velero)	boat (sail)
el bull dozer	bull dozer
el caballo mecedor	rocking horse
la caja de arena	sandbox
la caja de juguetes	toy box
la caja de pinturas	paint box
el camión	truck
el volquete	dump truck
el camión de los bomberos	fire truck
el camión de basura	garbage truck
el camión de aceite	oil truck

Toys

la canica	marble
la caña de pescar	fishing rod
la carretilla	wheelbarrel
el carretón	wagon
la casa de muñecas	doll house
el coche	car
el coche de carreras	race car
el cohete	rocket ship
el collar	necklace
el columpio	swing
la comba	jump rope
la cometa	kite
el computador	computer
el crayón	crayon
el cubo	block
la cuerda	rope
el engrudo	paste
el fuerte	fort
el globo	balloon
el globo	globe
la grúa	tow truck
cl helicóptero	helicopter
el indio	Indian
el jeep	jeep
el juego	game
el juego de té	tea service
el libro de colorear	picture book
el maniquí	puppet
la máscara	mask
el monopatín	skateboard
la muñeca	doll
el osito	teddy bear
la pala	shovel
el patín	skate
el patinete	skooter
el payaso	clown
la pelota	ball
el pincel	paint brush
el pito	whistle
la plasticina	clay

Toys

la raqueta de tenis	tennis racquet
el rastrillo	rake
el rompecabezas	puzzle
el sonajero	rattle
el soldadito (de plomo)	soldier (lead)
el soldadito (de madera)	soldier (wooden)
el sube y baja	see-saw
el submarino	submarine
el tablero de ajedrez	chess board
el tambor	drum
el tanque (militar)	tank (military)
las tijeras	scissors
la tienda de campaña	tent
el tobogán	slide
el tractor	tractor
el tren (eléctrico)	train (electric)
el triciclo	tricycle
el trineo	sled
la trompeta	horn
el trompo	top
el vaquero	cowboy
el xilófono	xylophone

Clothing

el abrigo	coat
el babero	bib
la bata de baño	bathrobe
la bata de dormir	nightgown
el blue jean	jeans
la blusa	blouse
la bota	boot
la bota de goma	rubber boot
la bufanda	scarf
el calcetín	sock

Clothing

la camisa	shirt
la camiseta	tee-shirt
la camiseta	undershirt
la cartera	pocketbook
la carterita	wallet
el cazoncillo	underpants
la chaqueta	jacket
la corbata	tie
el cordón (de zapato)	shoelace
la cremallera	zipper
las enaguas	slip
la falda	skirt
la gorra	cap
el guante	glove
el impermeable	raincoat
la media	stocking
las medias	tights
el mitón	mitten
la mochila	backpack
el overol	overalls
los pantalones	slacks
los pantalones cortos	shorts
el pañuelo	handkerchief
el paraguas	umbrella
el pijama	pajamas
la ropa interior	underwear
la sandalia	sandal
el sombrero	hat
el suéter	sweater
el traje de baño	bathing suit
el traje de nieve	snow suit
el vestido	dress
el zapato	shoe
(de tacón alto)	(high heel)
el zapato de tenis	sneaker
la zapatilla	slipper

The Human Body

la barbilla	chin
la boca	mouth

The Human Body

el brazo	arm
la cabeza	head
la cadera	hip
la cara	face
la ceja	eyebrow
la cintura	waist
el codo	elbow
el cuello	neck
el dedo	finger
el dedo (del pie)	toe
el diente	tooth
la espalda	back
el estómago	stomach
la frente	forehead
la garganta	throat
el hombro	shoulder
el labio	lip
la lengua	tongue
la mano	hand
la mejilla	cheek
la muñeca	wrist
la nariz	nose
el ojo	eye
el ombligo	belly button
la oreja	ear
la panza	tummy
el párpado	eyelid
el pecho	chest
el pelo	hair
el pie	foot
la pierna	leg
el pulgar	thumb
la quijada	jaw
la rodilla	knee
el talón	heel
el tobillo	ankle
el trasero	backside
la uña	fingernail

Beverages

el agua	water
(con hielo)	(with ice)
café (con leche)	coffee (with milk)
la cerveza	beer
el chocolate (caliente)	cocoa (hot)
Coca-Cola	Coca-Cola
la gaseosa de limón	lemon soda
el jugo de naranja	orange juice
la leche	milk
la limonada	lemonade
la naranjada	orangeade
el refresco (de uva, de naranja)	soda (grape, orange)
la soda	soda (club soda)
el té (una taza de)	tea (cup of)
el té (con limón)	tea (with lemon)
el vino	wine
el vino blanco	white wine

Desserts

el budín	pudding
el budín de arroz	rice pudding
el (cono de) helado	ice cream (cone)
el dulce	candy
el flan	custard
el flan de caramelo	caramel custard
el flan de chocolate	chocolate custard
el flan de vainilla	vanilla custard
la galletita	cookie
la gelatina	gelatin
el panqueque	pancake
el pastel de ...	pastry
la tarta de manzana	apple pie
la torta	cake
la torta de mantequilla	pound cake
el yogurt	yoghurt

Vegetables

el ajo	garlic
el apio	celery
la berenjena	eggplant
el bretón	Brussel sprout
el brócoli	broccoli
la calabaza	pumpkin
la cebolla	onion
el champiñon	mushroom
el choclo	(ear of) corn
el coliflor	cauliflower
el espárrago	asparagus
la espinaca	spinach
el guisante	pea
la judia verde	stringbean
la lechuga	lettuce
el maíz	corn
el nabo	turnip
el pepino	cucumber
el perejil	parsley
el pimentón	pepper
el rábano	radish
la remolacha	beet
el repollo	cabbage
el tomate	tomato
la zanahoria	carrot
el zapallo	squash

Meat

el bistek	steak
la chuleta de cerdo	pork chop
la chuleta de cordero	lamb chop
la hamburguesa	hamburger
el jamón	ham
la pata del cordero	leg of lamb
el pavo	turkey
el perrito caliente	hot dog
el pollo	chicken
la salchicha	sausage
el tocino	bacon

Seafood

el atún	tuna
el arenque	herring
el bacalao	cod
el camarón	shrimp
la carpa	carp
la langosta	lobster
el lenguado	sole
el pejerrey	flounder
el salmón	salmon
la sardina	sardine
la trucha	trout

Fruits

el albaricoque	apricot
la cereza	cherry
la ciruela	plum
la ciruela seca	prune
el coco	coconut
el durazno	peach
la frambuesa	raspberry
la fresa	strawberry
el limón	lemon
la mandarina	tangerine
la manzana	apple
el mirtilo	blueberry
la naranja	orange
la pasa	raisin
la pera	pear
la piña	pineapple
el plátano	banana
la salsa de manzana	applesauce
la sandía	watermelon
la toronja	grapefruit
la uva	grape
las uvas (racimo de)	grapes (bunch)

Other Foods

el almíbar	syrup
el algodón de azúcar	cotton candy

Other Foods

el arroz	rice
la avena	oatmeal
el cereal	cereal
el chocolate	milk chocolate
el chocrut	sauerkraut
el cocido	stew
las conservas	jam
la crema	cream
el emparedado	sandwich
el encurtido	pickle
la ensalada	salad
los espaguetis	spaghetti
los fideos	noodle
la galleta	cracker
la goma de mascar	chewing-gum
el huevo	egg
el huevo frito	fried egg
el huevo duro	hard-boiled egg
los huevos revueltos	scrambled
la maní	peanut
la mantequilla	butter
la mantequilla de maní	peanut butter
la mermelada	jelly
la miel	honey
la miga	crumb
las palomitas de maíz	popcorn
el pan	bread
el pancillo	bun, roll
el panqueque	pancake
las papas fritas	French fries
el pimienta	pepper
el puré de papas	mashed potatoes
el queso	cheese
la sal	salt
la salsa	sauce, gravy
la salsa de tomate	ketchup
la sopa	soup
la tostada	toast
el vinagre	vinegar

Tableware

la azucarera	sugar bowl
la bandeja	tray
la botella	bottle
la cuchara	table spoon
la cucharita	teaspoon
el cuchillo	knife
la cremera	creamer
la fuente	platter
la jarra	pitcher
la mantel	tablecloth
la olla	pot
la olla pequeña	saucepan
el platito	saucer
el plato	plate
el plato de postre	dessert plate
el plato hondo	bowl
el sartén	pan, skillet
la servilleta	napkin
el sopero	soup plate
la taza	cup
el tenedor	fork
la tetera	kettle, teapot
el vaso	glass

Containers

la bolsa, el saco	bag
la botella	bottle
la caja	box
la caja de cartón	carton
el envoltorio	wrapper
la jarra	jar
la jaula	crate
la lata	can
el sobre	envelope
la tapa	top, cover
el tubo	tube

House

el baño	bathroom
el buzón	mailbox
la cerca	fence
el césped	grass, lawn
la chimenea	chimney
la cocina	kitchen
el comedor	dining room
el desván	attic
el dormitorio	bedroom
la escalera	stair
el escalón	step
el jardín	garden, yard
la pared	wall
el pasillo	hallway
el piso	floor
la puerta	gate, door
la puerta principal	front door
la puerta trasera	back door
la regadera	lawn sprinkler
la sala	living room
el salón se estar	den
el sótano	basement
el techo	roof, ceiling
la ventana	window

Dwellings

el apartamento	apartment
el búngalo	bungalow
la cabina	cabin
la casa de campo	country house
la casa rodante	house trailer
el condominio	condo
el hotel	hotel
la tienda de campaña	tent

Kitchen

la alacena	cupboard
la aspiradora	vacuum cleaner
el balde	pail
el batidor de huevo	egg beater
el batidor eléctrico	electric beater
la cera (para muebles)	furniture wax
el colador	strainer
el delantal	apron
el detergente	detergent
el embudo	funnel
la escoba	broom
la esponja	sponge
la estufa	stove
el fregadero	sink
el gabinete	cabinet
el gabinete de las escobas	broom closet
el (horno de) microondas	microwave (oven)
la lavaplatos	dish washer
la lavaropa	clothes washer
la máquina de coser	sewing machine
la máquina de escribir	typewriter
la mesa	table
el mostrador	counter
la nevera, heladera	refrigerator
la plancha	iron
el plomero	duster
el recogedor de basura	dust pan
el reloj	clock
la secadora	clothes dryer
la tabla de planchar	ironing board
el taburete	stool
el tostador	toaster
el trapo	dish, dust cloth

Bedroom

la alfombra	carpet
la almohada	pillow

Bedroom

la butaca	armchair
la cama	bed
la colcha	quilt
el colchón	mattress
la colgador	coat hanger
la cómoda	dresser
la cortina	curtain
la cubrecama	bedspread
el enchufe	plug/ outlet
el disco compacto	CD
el espejo	mirror
el estereo	stereo
la lámpara	lamp
la manta	blanket
la mecedora	rocking chair
la persiana	shutter, blind
la sábana	sheet
la silla	chair
el velador	night table
el visillo	shade

Living Room

el aire acondicionado	air-conditioner
la chimenea	fireplace
el cuadro	picture
el estante	book case
la grabadora	recorder
el piano	piano
la radio	radio set
el sofá	couch
el teléfono	telephone
el televisor	tele set
la video-grabadora	VCR

Bathroom

la aspirina	aspirin
la bañera	bathtub
el cepillo de dientes	toothbrush
la colonia	cologne
la crema de la cara	face cream
el esmalte de uñas	nail polish
la hoja de afeitar	razor blade
el inodoro	toilet bowl
el jabón	soap
el jabón de afeitar	shaving soap
el lápiz de labio	lipstick
el lavamanos	sink
la máquina de afeitar	electric razor
el papel higénico	toilet paper
la pasta de dientes	toothpaste
el perfume	perfume
el talco	powder
la toalla	bath towel
la toallita de la cara	face cloth

Entertainments

el acuario	aquarium
el baloncesto	basketball
el béisbol	baseball
el cine	movie
el cínema	movie theatre
el circo	circus
el concierto	concert
los deportes	sports
el fútbol	soccer
el fútbol americano	football
el juego de boleo	bowling
el partido	game, match
el museo	museum
la natación	swimming
el recreo	recess (at school)
el restaurante	restaurant
el zoológico, el zoo	zoo

Tools

los alicates	pliers
la carretilla	wheelbarrow
el clavo	nail
el cortacésped	lawn mower
la escalera	ladder
la escoba	broom
la espada	spade
la hacha	axe
la horca	pitch fork
la llama	trowel
la llave inglesia	wrench
la manguera	hose
el martillo	hammer
la pala	shovel
el papel de lijar	sandpaper
el rastrillo	rake
el serrucho	saw
las tijeras	scissors
el tornillo	screw
el tornillo de banco	vise
la tuerca	nut
el zapapico	pick

Along the Road

la acera	sidewalk
el aeropuerto	airport
el andén	sidewalk
aparcar	to park
el auto deportive	sports car
el autopista	expressway
la boca de agua para incendios	fire plug
el buzón	mailbox
la calle	street
el camino	road
el camión	truck
la camioneta	pick-up truck
la grúa	tow truck

Along the Road

el campo	field
la carretera	highway
el carro de nieve	snow mobile
la casa	house
la casa de los bomberos	fire house
la casilla del teléfono	telephone booth
la cerca	fence
el circulo de tráfico	traffic circle
el coche	car
la congestión de tráfico	traffic jam
(hacer) dedo	to hitch-hike
el edificio	building
el edificio de apartamentos	apartment building
el edificio de oficinas	office building
la esquina	corner
la estación de autobús	bus station
la estación de tren	train station
la fábrica	factory
el farol	street light
la iglesia	church
el lavadero de coches	car-wash
el limite de velocidad	speed limit
la motocicleta	moped
la moto	motorcycle
la oficina de correos	post office
el ómnibus (del colegio)	(school) bus
la panne	breakdown
la parada de autobús	bus stop
el peatón	pedestrian
el poste del teléfono	telephone pole
el puente	bridge
el riel	track (railroad)
la rueda reventada	flat tire

Along the Road

el semáforo	traffic light
la señal	sign post
el seto	hedge
el taxi	taxi
el tráfico	traffic
el tren	train
el tunel	tunnel
el van	van
la vía	lane

The Car

el acelerador	accelerator
la antena	antenna
el arranque automático	starter
el asiento	seat
la bocina	horn
el capó	hood
la cerradura	lock
el faro	headlight
los frenos	brakes
el gato	jack
la guantera	compartment
la ignición	ignition
el limpiaparabrisas	wiper
la llanta	tire
el maletero	trunk
la manecilla	door handle
la matrícula	license plate
el motor	engine
el parabrisas	windshield
el parachoques	bumper
el retrovisor	mirror (car)
la rueda	wheel
el tablero de instrumentos	dashboard
la ventana trasera	rear window
el visor	sunvisor
el volante	steeringwheel

Stores

el almacén	department store
el banco	bank
la carnicería	butcher shop
el depósito de madera	lumber yard
la estación de gasolina	gas station
la farmacia	drug store
la ferretería	hardware store
la floristería	florist (shop)
la joyería	jewelry store
la lavandería	cleaners, laundromat
la lechería	dairy store
el mercado	grocery, market
la mueblería	furniture store
la panadería	bakery
la peluquería	barber, beauty shop
la tienda de ropa	clothing store
el vivero	nursery
la zapatería	shoe store

Occupations

el (la) abogado (a)	lawyer
el acomodador	usher
la acomodadora	usherette
la ama de casa	housewife
el (la) astronauta	astronaut
el (la) bibliotecario (a)	librarian
el bombero	fireman
la camarera	waitress
el camarero	waiter
el (la) camionero (a)	truck driver
el (la) carnicero (a)	butcher
el (la) carpintero (a)	carpenter
el cartero	mailman
el chófer	chaufferur, taxi driver
el chófer de autobús	bus driver
el (la) cocinero (a)	cook
el (la) comerciante	merchant
el corredor automovilista	race car driver
el (la) criado (a)	servant
el cura	priest
el (la) dentista	dentist
el (la) doctor (a)	doctor
el (la) dueño (a) de la tienda	shop owner
el (la) enfermo (a)	nurse
el (la) farmaceútico (a)	pharmacist
el (la) granjero (a)	farmer
el (la) ingeniero (a) (de trenes)	engineer (train)
el (la) jardinero (a)	gardener
el joyero	jeweler
el (la) maestro(a)	teacher
el marinero	sailor
el (la) mecánico (a)	mechanic
el (la) modelo	model
el (la) niñerola	baby sitter
el (la) panadero(a)	baker
el piloto	pilot
el (la) pintor (a)	painter
el (la) policía	police
el rabino	rabbi
la secretaria	secretary
el serviente	servant
el (la) tendero (a)	grocer
el (la) técnico (a) de computador	computer technician
el vigilante del zoológico	zoo keeper

Animals

la ardilla	quirrel
la ballena	whale
el buey	ox
el burro	donkey
el caballo	horse
el caballito	pony
la cabra	goat
el camello	camel
el caniche	French poodle

Animals

la cebra	zebra
el cerdito	piglet
el cerdo	pig
el cervato	fawn
el ciervo	deer
el cocodrilo	crocodile
el cordero	lamb
el cornejo	rabbit
el cornejillo de Indias	guinea pig
la culebra	snake
el elefante	elephant
la foca	seal
el gato	cat
el gorila	gorilla
el gusano	worm (earth)
el hipopótamo	hipppotamus
la jirafa	giraffe
el león	lion
el leopardo	leopard
la llama	llama
el lobo	wolf
el mapache	raccoon
el mono	monkey
el oso	bear
la oveja	sheep
el pájaro	bird
el perrito	puppy
el perro	dog
la rana	frog
la rata	rat
el ratón	mouse
el reno	reindeer
el tigre	tiger
el topo	mole
el toro	bull
la tortuga	turtle
la vaca	cow
el zorro	fox

Birds

el águila	eagle
la alondra	lark
el avestruz	ostrich
el azulejo	bluebird
el canario	canary
el cardinal	cardinal
la cigueña	stork
el cisne	swan
el cuervo	raven, crow
el gallo	rooster
el gansarón	gosling
el ganso	goose
la gaviota	seagull
la golondrina	swallow
el gorrión	sparrow
la lechuza	owl
el loro	parrot
el mirlo	blackbird
el pájaro mosca	hummingbird
el pájaro carpintero	woodpecker
la paloma	pigeon, dove
el patito	duckling
el pato	duck
el pavo	turkey
el pavón	peacock
el pechicolorado	robin
el pelicano	pelican
el perico	parakeet
el pingüino	penguin
el pollito	chick
el pollo	chicken
el ruiséñor	nightingale

Insects

la abeja (de miel)	bee
el abejarrón	bumblebee
(la araña)	(spider)

Insects

la cigarra — cicada
el cortón — praying mantis
la cucaracha — cockroach
el grillo — cricket
la hormiga — ant
la libélula — dragonfly
la mariquita — lady bug
la mariposa — butterfly
el mosquito — mosquito
la mosca — fly
la oruga — caterpillar
la polilla — moth
la pulga — flea
el saltamontes — grasshopper

Trees

el abedul — birch
el abeto — hemlock
el álamo — poplar
el árbol frutal — fruit tree
el arce — maple
el cerezo — cherry
el ciruelo — plum
la encina — oak
el manzano — apple
la palmera — palm
el peral — pear
la picea — spruce
el pino — pine
el sauce — willow
la sequoia — sequoia

Flowers

la arveja olorosa — sweet pea
el azafrán — crocus
la azalea — azalea
la azucena — lily
el botón de oro — buttercup
el clavel — carnation
el crisántemo — chrysanthemum
la dalia — dahlia
el diente de león — dandelion
la estrella federal — poinsettia
la flor de lis — iris
la gardenia — gardenia
el geranio — geranium
el girasol — sunflower
la lila — lilac
el lirio de los valles — lily of the valley
la margarita — daisy
la mimosa — mimosa
el narciso — daffodil
el pensamiento — pansy
la peonía — peony
la petunia — petunia
la prímula — cowslip
el rododendro — rhododendron
la rosa — rose
el tulipán — tulip
la violeta — violet

PRONUNCIATION GUIDE

The following information on pronunciation is provided to answer basic questions which may arise regarding correct English pronunciation. Pronunciation for English is based on standard American usage. This means that the models given within this book will be understood and accepted throughout the country.

Unlike Spanish, English has a variety of sounds represented by the same letter. A letter in the same combination of letters is often pronounced differently. For example, the "i" in the word "drivers" is a long i. (It is the same sound as its name.) In the word "rivers," i has a short sound like the "i" in the English word "tin."

There can be as many as five different sounds for the same letter. Because of this possible variety, each English sentence in Kids Stuff Inglés includes pronunciation. (Because of space restraints, however, only one pronunciation is given in Kids Stuff Inglés.) Furthermore, a brief key to pronunciation is given below. It should be remembered that this key is only a basic representation of individual letters.

Note: An apostrophe (') is placed in many sentences where two words should be pronounced as if they were one for smoothness. For example, "to the store" should be pronounced,"t∪th∪stor."

VOWELS

Letter	Kids Stuff Symbol	English Words	Sound as in Spanish Words
A	a	hat, lap, happy	-------------
	ah	not, father	cada, nadar, cara
	ei	gate, game, they	rey, seis
E	ee	me, sea, fee	día, allí
	eh	care, hair, where	-------------
	e	head, let, get	el, es
	er	lower, after	-------------
I	i	fit, tin	------------
	igh	sigh, fry, pie	hay, maillot
O	oh	hope, soap, no	malo, lago
	aw	off, lost	------------
	oy	boy, toy	hoy, oiga
	aou	how, found	auto, trauma
U	oo	too, fool	un, luna
	u	foot, put, look, could	-----------
	uh	some, but, upon, aboard	------------
	ur	first, work	------------

CONSONANTS

B: as in Spanish

C: as in the Spanish words ***cinco***, or ***comer***

D: as in the Spanish word ***dónde.***

F: as in Spanish ***fantástico.***

G: as ***g*** in the Spanish word ***gato***.

H: as ***j*** in the Spanish word ***jefe.***

J: English ***j*** is similar to Spanish ***ch.***

K: as ***c*** in the Spanish word ***cama.***

L: as in Spanish.

M: as in Spanish.

N: as in Spanish.

P: as ***p*** in the Spanish word ***partido.***

Q: always followed by ***u*** and has the sound of English "***kw***."

R: the sound between Spanish ***r*** and ***rr***.

S: as in the Spanish word ***casa.***

T: as in Spanish.

V: the sound produced with the upper front teeth on the lower lip.

W: similar to the initial sound in the Spanish word ***huevo***.

X: similar to the sound of the Spanish ***j.***

Y: similar to the sound of the Spanish ***ll.***

Z: a buzzing sound similar to the ***s*** in Spanish.

INDEX

C

C

D

D

E

H

I

J

L

M

N

O

P

P

P

Q

R

R

S

CUT, COLOR *and* PASTE

A colorful, fun and easy way to get acquainted with this book is to match the pictures with the sentences in the text. The page number on the back of each drawing is given to help you spot the page you are looking for. An asterisk next to the appropriate sentence is also given to help you pinpoint the exact sentence. Sometimes a picture will match more than one sentence.

Bingo –

These pages can be used to play Bingo reenforcing learned English vocabulary and, of course, just for fun.

Look on pages 13 – 27 and match
these pictures with the correct sentences.

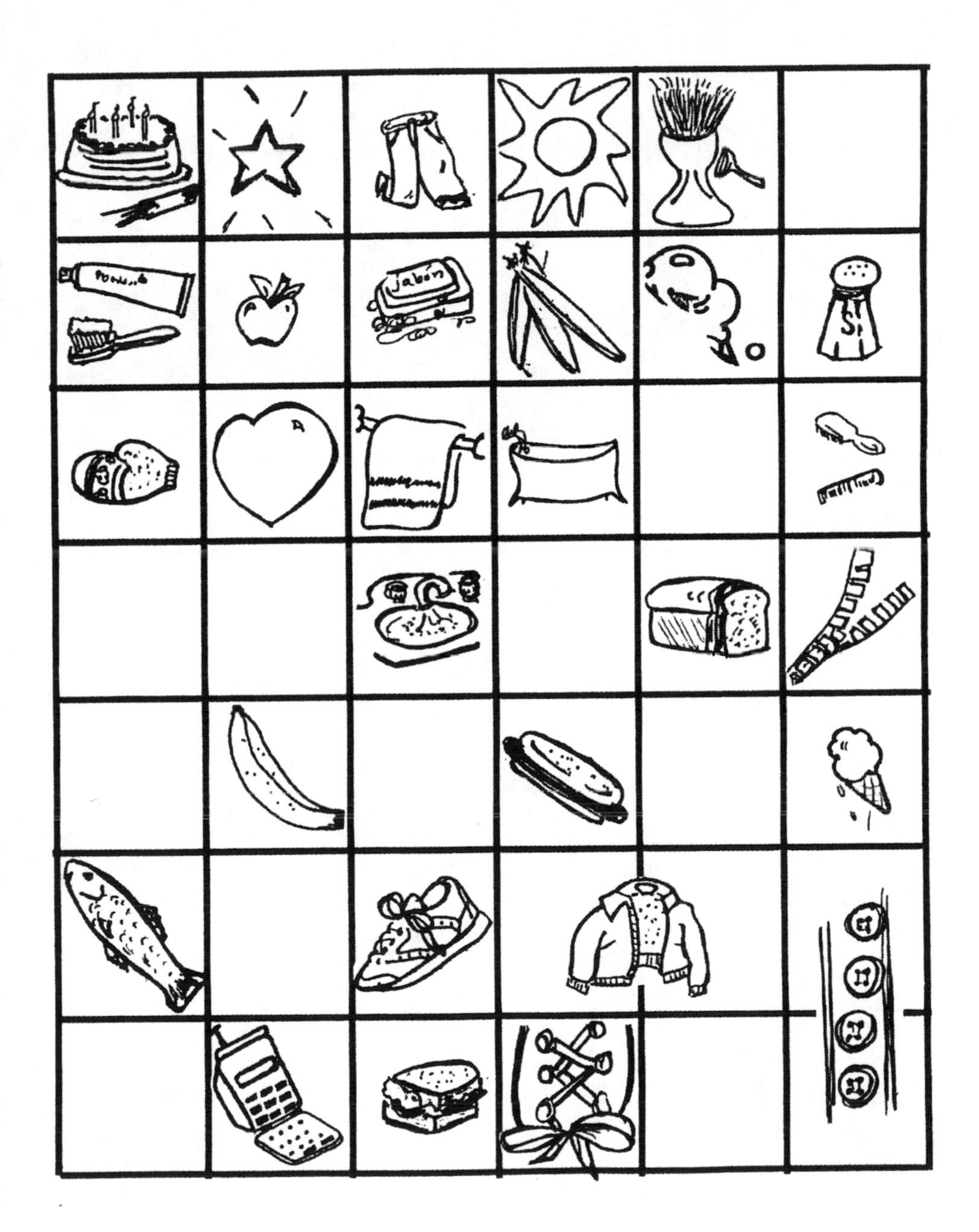

19 15 20 15 15

25 18 26 18 25 17

22 18 18 14 21

21 27 17

26 25 25

21 20 26

21

22 24 13

Look on pages 29 – 53 and match
these pictures with the correct sentences.

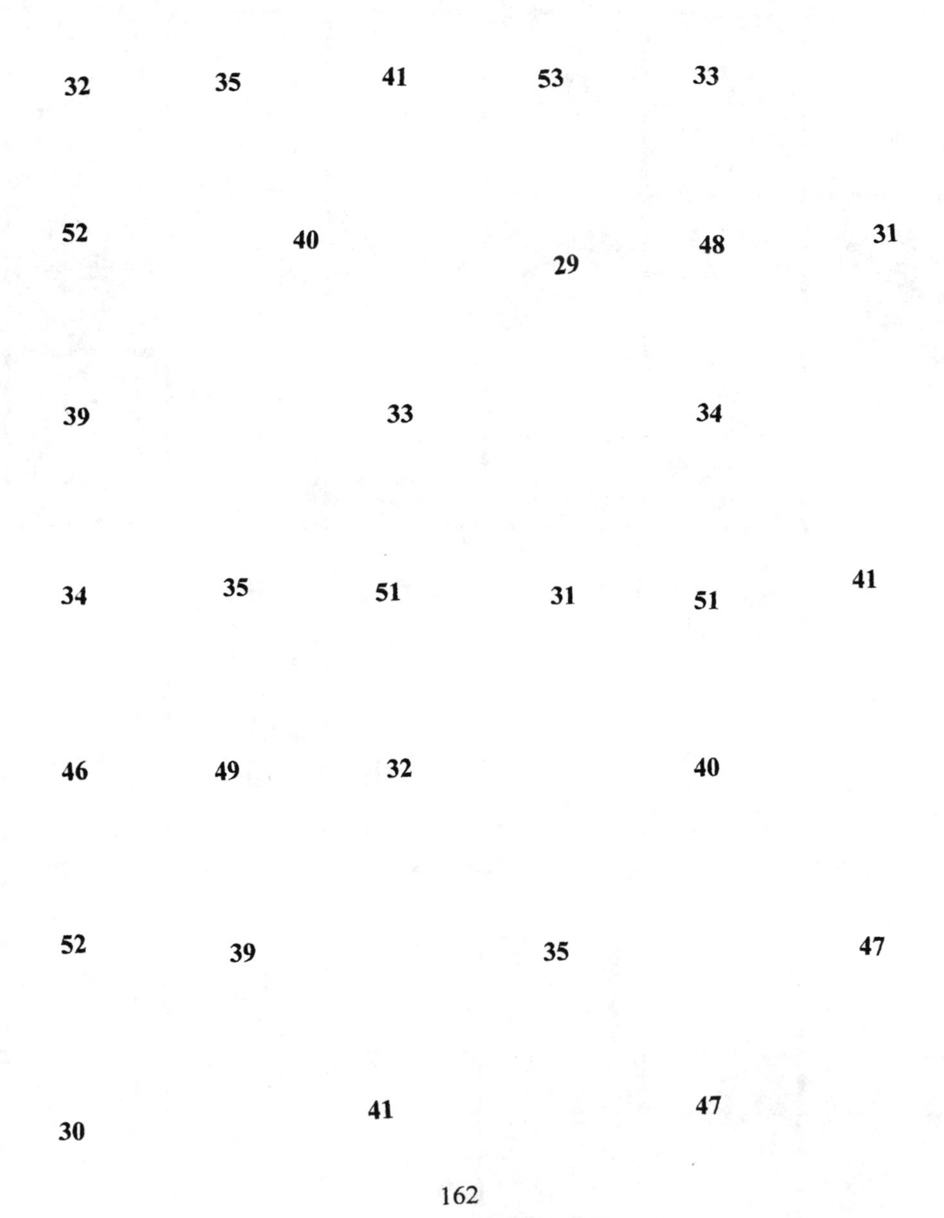
32
35
41
53
33
52
40
29
48
31
39
33
34
34
35
51
31
51
41
46
49
32
40
52
39
35
47
30
41
47

Look on pages 54 – 79 and match these pictures with the correct sentences.

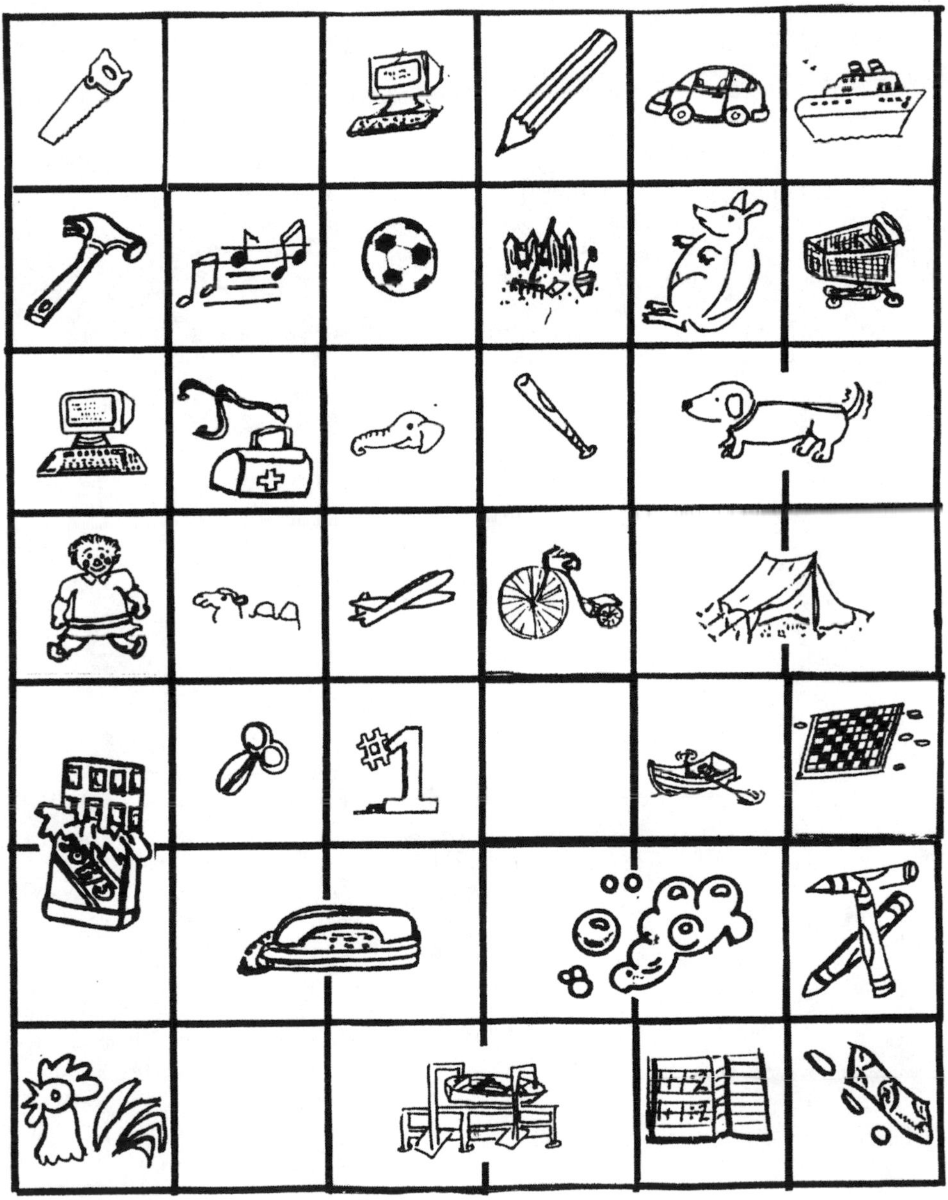

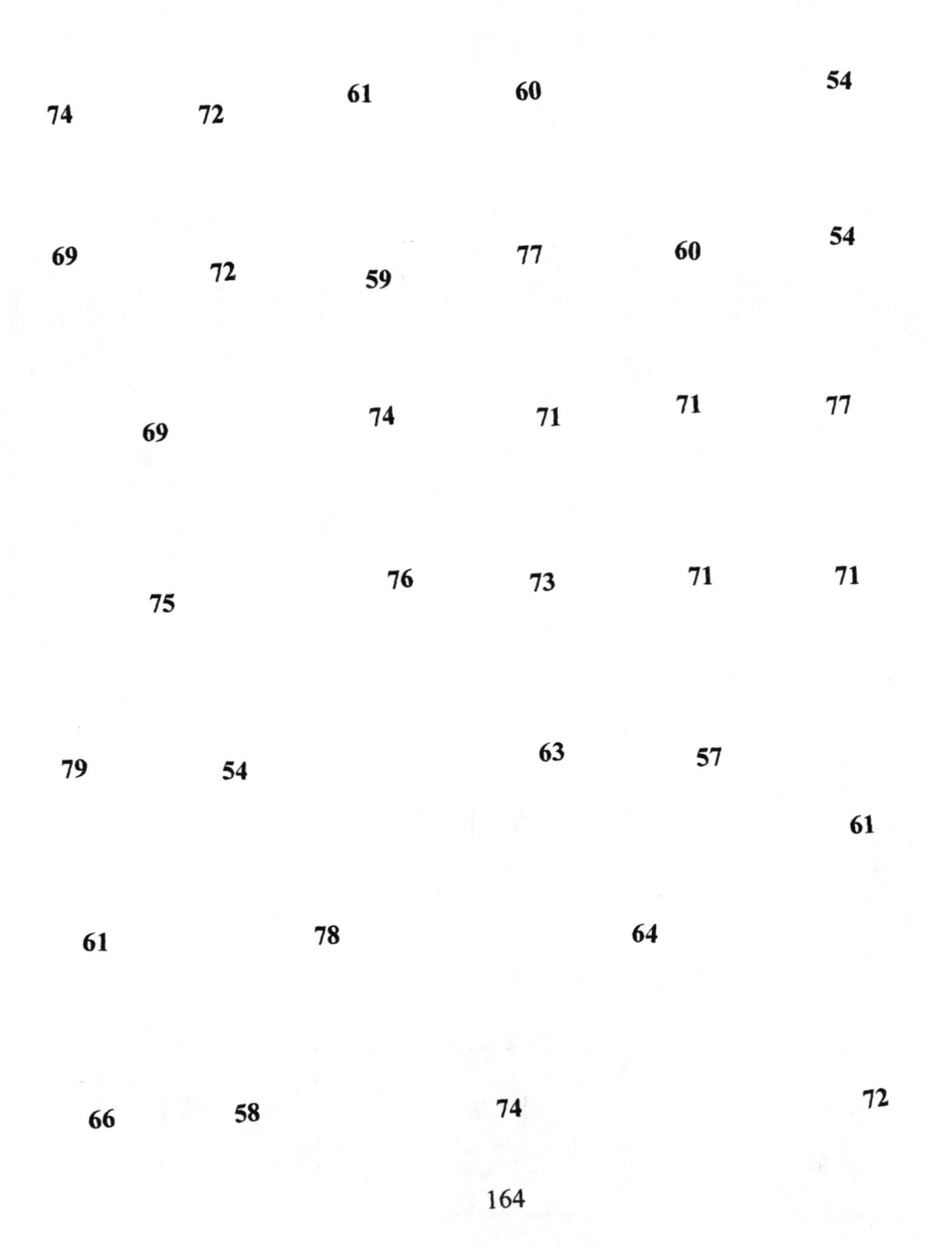
74
72
61
60
54
69
72
59
77
60
54
69
74
71
71
77
75
76
73
71
71
79
54
63
57
61
61
78
64
66
58
74
72

Look on pages 80 – 110 and match
these pictures with the correct sentences.

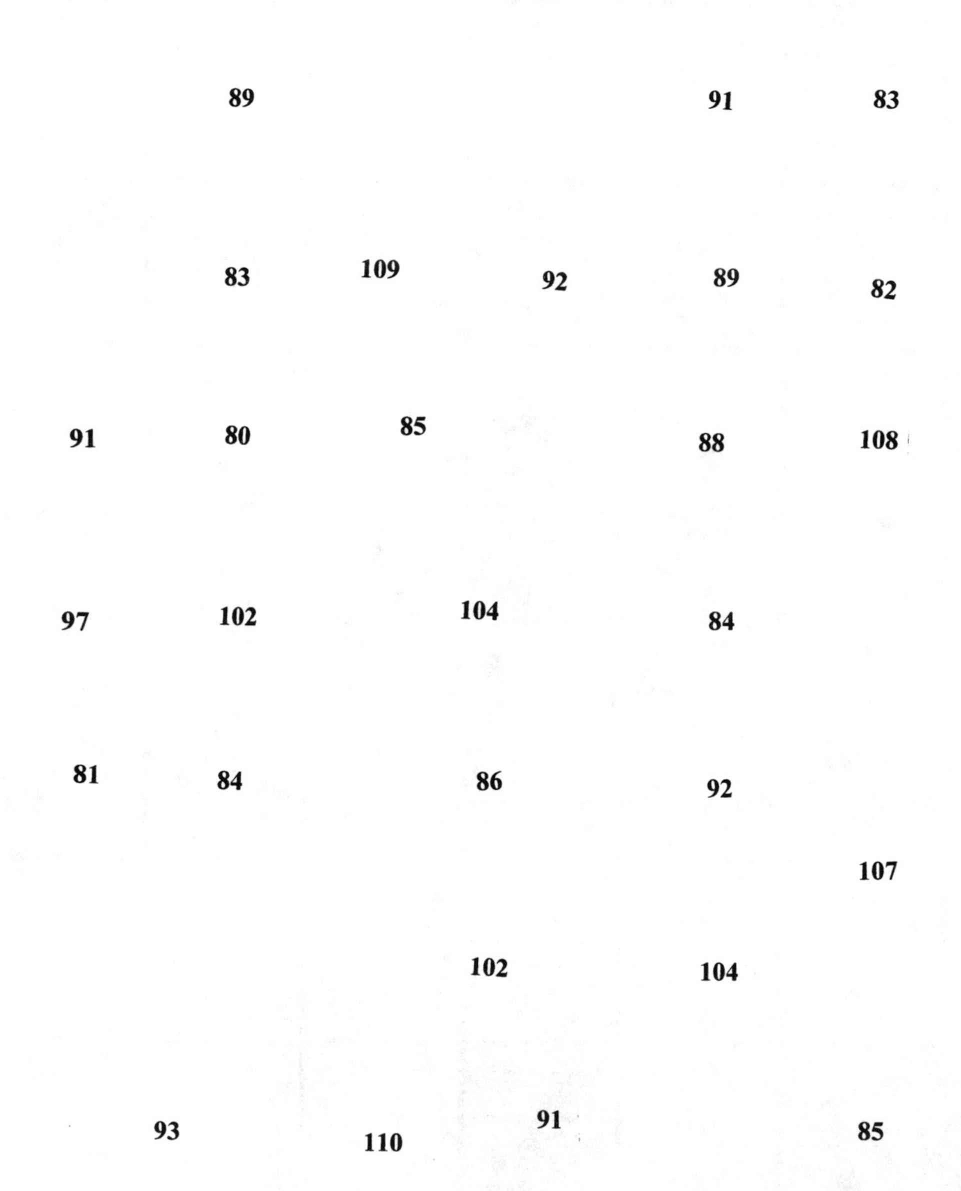
89
91
83
83
109
92
89
82
91
80
85
88
108
97
102
104
84
81
84
86
92
107
102
104
93
110
91
85

Books from Chou Chou Press ---

Bilingual Kids Series:

Kids Stuff **Italian**

Kids Stuff **Spanish**

Kids Stuff **German**

Kids Stuff **French**

Kids Stuff **Russian**

Kids Stuff **Inglés**

Kids Stuff **Angliiski (English)**

ABC's of SAT's: How One Student Scored a Perfect 800 on the Verbal SAT (A comprehensive reading list for children)

BILINGUAL KIDS SERIES